Faith That Doesn't Burn

By Steven Bornbach

Contact information for this book

For copies of this book or to find it as an e book go to:
faithburn@solarus.net

Contact information:

Steven Bornbach

2340 Chestnut Street,

Wisconsin Rapids, Wisconsin 54494

Design by Griffon Graphics

ISBN 978-1-5323-1329-5
1 3 5 7 9 10 8 6 4 2

To My Parents:

I wish to thank my mother who tried to teach me right from wrong while I was growing up. As Merle Haggard said in one of his songs, "momma tried, momma tried."

I wish to thank my father for leading me to eternal life and who in my adulthood has more than made up for my childhood. Dad also taught me that, "There are certain traits that are handed down through the generations; some are good, some are bad. The good ones we cultivate, the bad ones we break the curse."

Contents

Author's note

Prologue

Chapter one: Past and Present are Intertwined

Chapter two: In the Beginning

Chapter three: Corn Flakes and Cold Tar

Chapter four: Roles People Play in Our Development

Chapter five: Elementary and Grade School

Chapter six: Fire and Water

Chapter seven: The Dry Run

Chapter eight: Neighbors

Chapter nine: A Fork in the Road

Chapter ten: Darkness is Falling

Chapter eleven: Drugs and More Drugs

Chapter twelve: God Works in Mysterious ways

Chapter thirteen: A New Creation

Chapter fourteen: For the Skeptics

Chapter fifteen: Would You Like to Know Jesus?

Chapter sixteen: Faith that Doesn't Burn

Steven Bornbach

Introduction

Steve Bornbach was a simple country boy growing up in central Wisconsin, U.S.A. Growing up in the beautiful township of Saratoga afforded many memorable stories; such as dirt track races, hillbillies on go carts, voices of 'women' screaming in the night, wasps making music on hot summer days, a dry run full of water, fighting against snapping turtles, and much more.

Teenage years became filled with loneliness, rejection, and pain, which became a catalyst for making wrong choices. This resulted in Steve becoming ensnared in a web of drugs and crime causing him to question what life is all about. What is faith and what do we put our faith in? God had a plan for Steve's life and he has a plan for your life. Come take a journey with, "Faith that Doesn't Burn."

Steven Bornbach

Author's Note

This memoir is based on events beginning before the time I was born and which culminated in my late teens. I have tried to tell my story truthfully. For the sake of transparency, I have chosen to use distinct events, dialogue and sequence of events, to tell my own one of a kind story. Some names and details have been changed to protect privacy of individuals.

Steven Bornbach

I'd like to acknowledge an influential person in my life. Janet Hoff was my third grade instructor. Her patience, guidance, and influence have impacted this project. Janet- I am proud to call you a friend.

- Steve

Steven Bornbach

Prologue

This is an autobiography. What you are about to read is not fiction - the events actually happened. It is not the intent of this author to glorify or condone wrong behaviors; however, in being "real", some stories will be quite gritty. While portions of this material might be funny, please keep in mind that certain segments will touch on topics such as sex, drugs and crime. Therefore, children should not have access to these stories without parental supervision.

This work was begun over twenty five years ago, and it has been a slow random work in progress. A few stories may appear more than once, sometimes from my point of view as victim and sometimes my point of view as the perpetrator. Since this work began, my views have changed over the years and the need to take ownership for my mistakes has become important to me.

The world often stereotypes "Christians" as boring, straight laced squares who do not have a clue about life in the real world. I suppose there truly are people like that in churches; however, many of us "have done it all." We know what we were and what we are, sinners, saved only by grace.

People may ask, why bring up the past? Sometimes one has to bring up the past to bring about closure. Long buried hurts that you may have forgotten often remain deep inside, causing turmoil. I had problems with relationships as an adult until I realized how something from the past was still affecting me. Once I dealt with a past event, the problem was resolved. Another question people ask is, why share the past with others? Well, imagine how empty libraries and book stores would be if no one ever wrote biographies, autobiographies or self-help books based on their experiences. From our failures and victories we learn empathy for others; when we share our experiences with other hurting people, we earn the right to become their friend and perhaps help them.

1

Chapter One

Past and Present are Intertwined

I have experienced several self-revelations about myself since my divorce. These Revelations pertain to how one's early life and child hood disposition cement and impact future events such as marriage, divorce, desires, convictions and the driving force behind what we do and who we are. Many times as I look back and write, I say such things as "this contributed to ...."

I have found a niche in my life - Genealogy, writing, history and geography, which are all consuming. This craving, this itch which must be scratched, is an all-consuming fire which is a tool to be used in the grand scheme of things for a divine eternal purpose. This niche, if you will, is nothing new. It began as a young boy growing up in the fifth grade. There are many chapters that make up a person's life, and as one grows older, it becomes evident how the pieces begin to fit together. My thoughts looking back into childhood are often fast forwarded into the present in a pronounced and profound way. The past was a foundation poured in childhood, a foundation unseen, which lay dormant and was not built upon until later in life when conditions became favorable.

Life often ends much the same as it began. We enter the world small and helpless and we go out of this world old and feeble. In the beginning we swim away from birth and in the end we swim into death. It is said that a salmon swims back to the place where its life first began as it senses its life is about to end. For me, my life of early childhood began when I was delivered at Overview Hospital in Grand Rapids, Wisconsin. We then lived upstairs for the next four years of my life, on the second floor of an apartment at the home of Mrs. July Pech on South Street in Appaloosa, Wisconsin.

In 1963, we moved onto Strangeline Road, three miles east of Appaloosa, Wisconsin. It was here that my preschool years were spent mainly with my mother and siblings. Social interaction was solely between my siblings and me and not with the outside world. Eventually a new chapter unfolded, the period of entering school and an awareness of the outside world. Later I will allude to what I refer to as being pushed into Kindergarten early. That plan backfired as I sat outside on the playground swings long after recess was over.

As a youngster I craved attention. I had the ability to both knowingly and unknowingly irritate both teachers and boys of the older grades. I suppose I welcomed abuse by being different, and the more I was persecuted and beaten, the more I taunted those who abused me. My taunting might well be classified as "smarting off" – all to get attention. Many times older boys wanted to "pound on me," and as I ran to get away, I would look over my shoulder and yell, "You can't catch me"! They were furious.

The "persecution" or social hardships, if you will, followed me all through school. I'm sure God gave me my special personality as a child to temper me and make me strong for the trials I am to face in the future, for being a born again follower of Jesus Christ. I am conditioned to speak out against what I see as wrong even when that may be unpopular. As an adult, there were many times in the mid-1980s when my wife would tell me that I could not write Letters to the Editor because she was worried what others might think. I am not always right, but I have always spoken my convictions with no regrets, after all, that's who I am.

As to the bullies chasing me, they may have not been able to catch me on the playground, but, unfortunately, the same boys rode the bus with me on my way home after school. Those older kids who always sat all the way back on the bus suddenly were surrounding me in the middle of the bus, socking me in the guts while making threats.

My mother graciously allowed me to join the Cub Scouts when I was in second grade and that lasted for three weeks. The same boys who had it in for me out on the playground and on the bus were also the same fellows in the cub den. It was no surprise when I walked into the house one day and saw my mother sobbing while she was listening to the den mother on the other end of the phone line. I was banned from Cub Scouts, and that was how life went for me all through school.

Today was May 5, 2015, and as I read the obituaries in the paper I found the name of one of my former tormenters; he was 56. Not only did he try to make my life miserable as a child, but he also tried to do the same as an adult. His glass was only half full throughout life and he was not exactly filled with joy. Knowing Ben, I would not be surprised if he had ended his life by suicide. His life was so barren. He was a God hater; a hater of Christ's followers, never happy with his employers, just misery. Perhaps his family saw something positive in him that somehow escapes me, but I fear he went out into eternity without Christ and the rewards Jesus gives to those who are faithful to Him. I am deeply sorry that Ben did not appear to live a rich life of fullness.

In viewing child hood, the past regularly flashes forward into the present. As our life goes on, walls of other rooms or compartments are being built into the house of our life. We keep going back to the foundation of what we are building upon. The reason I say all of this is because many decades later as an adult, I have gone back to right wrongs. For anyone I have angered, or offended or cheated, I have tried to make right by them and offered my hand of friendship. I have few takers for my friendship. Maybe that is due in part to the busyness of everyone's lives. I suppose I could feel bad and ask myself what is wrong with me, but I know there is nothing wrong. It is my goal to have as little as possible standing between God and me when I stand before Him on judgment day.

Going back to my childhood, my favorite subjects were science and history. I did not hate school nor did I love it. I suppose I put up with it. I was always happy to go home at the end of each day. Oh, I did not have a perfect home to go to, but at home, I had ways of amusing myself. I was excited to go home each day to black and white television, to mud puddles, ants, the smell of mowed grass, yellow – white pine pitch on trees along with all the rest of what you find in nature.

Nature, for me, was water running through the muddy gravel driveway as it ran towards the road as the snow melted in the spring. My greatest enjoyment was to make channels and dams for the water, diverting flows and analyzing my impact on the waters path from source to puddle. That very same water would again freeze overnight making very thin sheets of ice over the large puddles. It was always an adventure before the bus came, to walk out onto the ice and watch the spider webbing as the ice cracked under my weight. It was an adrenaline rush to edge out across the ice wondering when I was going to break through. This was all wonderful entertainment while waiting for the school bus to pick me up.

As I stood by the road in the early morning, I could hear the heralding of the song birds – black capped chickadees, robins, cardinals, blue jays, crows, rose breasted grosbeaks. It was as if they were all serenading me. Of course I now know that all of those birds were singing their mating calls back and forth to one another. As I listened to the birds, my eyes were feasted to a view of the sun's rays hitting the very tippy tops of the tall jack pines across the road, to the north of Mr. Flintstone's house.

I could feel Mr. Sunshine on the back of my neck as he rose over our house in back of me. Higher and higher he rose ever so slowly. As the sunlight increased, I could feel the warmth move down my back as this happened. The light on top of the jack pines across the road would move slowly down the trees, dissipating the shadows. Oh, I know it sounds quite remarkable that the sun could do so much in the time that I was waiting for my bus, but one must remember that the sun quickly rises much the same as it quickly sets in the twilight of the day.

I loved playing outside, playing in the dirt, playing in the woods, and making forts with the neighbor boys as they played Daniel Boone. Yes, Daniel Boone was a big hit on TV at that time, so everyone would run around the woods playing cowboys and Indians. In my excitement, I would lose track of time even as the night fell. My parents would yell out the back door for me to come into the house to get cleaned up and ready for bedtime. For some reason, I was so preoccupied with the fun of the great outdoors that I would not go into the house when I was supposed to.

One night, my parents called for me three times to get into the house, and that was the last time that I disobeyed when they called for me. I remember being grabbed as I walked through the door that evening and having the seat of my pants warmed by my father's hand. As I looked in the bathroom mirror, I could see that my right cheek was black and blue. There would be two other times in my life when I would get spankings like that. Once a year later when I received an "F" on my report card, and that was because I needed glasses and could not see the blackboard. Then ten years later, I was spanked with a 2x4 piece of lumber for throwing tomatoes at cars. Were my spankings child abuse? Well, maybe they were excessive, but Dad never had a wholesome role model when he was growing up, so I do not blame him. How could he know any better? Society at that time believed strongly in corporal punishment. In Catholic schools, spankings were acceptable and the public schools were not any better. I was slapped in the face, beat on the fingers by rulers and choked by different teachers numerous times, from kindergarten through fourth grade.

As I was in my childhood, so I have been in adulthood. Like my imperfect father, and like his imperfect father, I have made mistakes over the years.

Had I gone into the house at night to spend more time with my wife perhaps I would still be married. Just as I was preoccupied with the building of forts and playing during my childhood, so I was consumed with a sense of urgency to provide for my family. I had to get the wood ready for winter, get the garden harvested for food and get the lawn mowed. I often mowed in the dark with light from the street lamp before the lawn could be too long to mow. Yes, some lessons I never learned and never will learn. My musings and writings constantly take me from past to present. I regularly look over my life at the way I was and at who I am today. In my early formative years maybe I was a bit of a misfit and a screw-up. Just last year I met a former classmate by the name of Mick Fresh. I had been working on Mick's family history because it parallels mine. Mick of course did not know what I was doing, as we had not met for nearly forty years. I went to Mick's house one day; I introduced myself to his wife. I told her that Mick hated me when we attended school. Mick looked me in the eye and said to me, "I did not hate you. You were just different." Well there you have it, I was different. I want to say that I thank God for the opportunity to have met Mick as an adult. He is a great guy and I have mountains of respect for him.

I was different, yes I guess that described me, but let me tell you the way I was different. I was different because I would see without seeing and hear without hearing. I cannot explain it. I did not seem to see and hear what other people would see and hear. On the other hand, I would see and hear the things that other people did not see or hear. One example of this goes back to the day of my first communion.

What happened on first communion day went as follows. Our first communion class was sitting in the pews at the front on the left side of the church. I remember we were sitting or kneeling and the kids to my left were whispering something to one another. When the message was passed on to me, I quickly passed the message to the kids on my right, that after the ceremony we were to meet in the parochial school across the parking lot for photographs. After the ceremony, I remember having to go to the bathroom. I headed downstairs to the basement of the church to where the bathrooms were. Upon leaving the bathroom, I found the church to be deserted. I ran outside and looked toward the school but no one was around. I totally forgot about where the communion pictures were to be taken. I wandered down the sidewalk toward down town half a mile away, wondering where everyone could be. I made it as far as the Wisconsin River Bridge and then I started heading back north toward the church.

I was at the intersection of Prospect and Fifth Street, which was three blocks south of church, when my dad pulled up in the car and asked what I was doing. The photographer had waited as long as he could before taking pictures and of course I was not in them. Imagine my embarrassment trying to explain to my parents, grandparents and relatives what had happened.

Imagine the embarrassment I caused for my parents and relatives while all of those people were waiting. This was the story of my life while growing up, not really hearing or perhaps spacing out. This turned out to be another problem in my marriage because I was accused of having selective hearing.

Today, forty five years later, I still struggle to hear or understand what other people are saying. Many times my children would try to explain a point to me but I had tunnel vision and could not connect with what they were trying to say. Sometimes, the light would come on in my brain and in the next day, week or month I would finally realize what others were trying to say to me. This is very frustrating for me.

My love of history began in my child hood during fifth and sixth grade. Studying American history, the lives of American presidents and reading about pioneers of our country was very exciting for me. Memorizing the fifty states along with their capitals and learning geography also made me quite happy. Libraries have held a very special place in my heart. As an eleven, twelve and thirteen year old, I would check out biographies of frontiersmen who tamed this great country, those who transformed it into a great nation. There were Ethan Allen and the Green Mountain boys, Davy Crockett, Daniel Boone, Jim Bowie, John Jacob Astor and others I remember. There were also historical events such as the Battle of the Alamo and the conquering of the West as pioneers moved westward.

I rushed from the bus each day after school and headed towards my bedroom to read the books of adventure. I lay with my back on the bed and with my head on a pillow, and I would read by the light of a window until it was too dark to see. The biographical events of others transported me back in time, to a more appealing period in history from which I have never really departed. As I became a teenager, my other form of relaxing became fishing and spending time outdoors. It would not be long, however, before those days of adolescence would become filled with dark unwholesome activities.

Steven Bornbach

2

Chapter Two

In the Beginning

My father graduated from high school in the spring of 1955. He began working at the mobile home plant in Stratford, Wisconsin, several miles from where he grew up on Oxbow Road, north of Daul Town. During that time all he had to drive was an old Harley Davidson motorcycle. One day in November, he went to ride his bike to work with his buddy, Art, riding on the back. They became stuck in a snow drift by Spindler's farm on Hwy. M and were so weary of winter that they decided to enlist in the Navy together; by January of 1956 Dad was at Great Lakes Naval Academy.

In the navy, Dad worked in sections of the engine room on the air craft carrier, "Forrestal," as the ship made tours through the Mediterranean Sea in Europe. Upon honorable discharge from active duty in November of 1957, Dad went looking for work in North Dakota. Alvin, Dad's oldest brother, drove out there in a 42 Dodge, and the two also brought along Grandpa John Bornbach. The men had hopes of finding employment by digging potatoes during harvest time, but they were too late and harvest was over.

The next trip Dad and Alvin made together was to Iowa to harvest the fall corn crop for animal feed. This lasted for about a month. With a little money that was saved and with a small loan from Dad's sister, Allie, Dad was able to make a down payment on a 1957 Chevy. This took place around the first of the year in 1958. Afterwards, Dad began working at the Roddis Company in Cashfield (later called Weyerhaeuser). Since Dad now worked in Cashfield, it was decided that he would car pool his mother Eleanor and her co – worker, Miss Gee, to work at the Cashfield hospital each day. This went on for the better part of a year. Dad was in Daul Town at the Kraut House Tavern one day when Miss Gee walked in all dressed up. They began dating that summer and were married in May of 1959. One day Miss Gee met a patient at the hospital by the name of Rosie Greer. Rosie informed Miss Gee that Appaloosa Papers was hiring people who would be interested in working for the mill. Dad applied that April of 1959 and the next day was hired, eventually becoming a millwright. During the first couple of months, Dad lived with Rosie just west of Appaloosa at the intersection of Wood Avenue and Highway 173. He stayed there until he had enough money to rent a place of his own. The first home my parents had, was in an upstairs apartment owned by Mrs. July Pech on South Street in Appaloosa. Here is where my life story begins.

I was born in 1959 entering this world several weeks early. I was born to a young millwright named David Bornbach and his wife, Miss Gee. Dad had been recently hired as an employee of Appaloosa Papers. The town was made up of approximately 2000 people and was located 40 miles from where each of my parents had been living. My mother actually grew up in Chicago on Florence Street and worked as a backhoe operator while attending high school. Upon graduation, her family moved back up north to the old family homestead in Daul Town, Wisconsin.

I was born the oldest of five children. I had four siblings who lived and two sisters that were Siamese twins who died at birth. We were all very close in age as seven of us were born in five years. My one sibling and I are 362 days apart in age and when her birthday occurs each year, we are the same age for three days. Mom was very busy as a result of so many children in such a short time span, she never had any rest. There was constant cleaning, cloth diapers constantly being laundered, and of course Dad had to have his supper on the table at 3:40 every day when he walked in the door from work. To make life even more challenging, Mom had to divide her time attending to the needs of five children. Hearing our pleas, breaking up squabbles, preparing us for kindergarten, and of course picking up everything that we messed up. Consequently, there was not much time for one on one interaction, yet she found time to teach me how to tie my shoes, count to ten, and learn the alphabet. When it was bedtime, she taught me prayers and before I went to sleep, we prayed as follows: Guardian angel of God, my guardian dear, to whom His love commits me here, ever this day be at my side, to light and guard and rule and guide.

My siblings and I were always in a group, whether it was for a field trip and picnic to the zoo or to the airport to watch airplanes. We took trips to Daul Town to visit grandparents nearly every week-end. Dad was not around much to help Mom because of his strong work ethic; he had a young family to support, so it was work, work, and more work. We never had a father son relationship while I was grow-ing up. I doubt we spoke 300 words a year to each other. We never threw a football, played catch or bas-ketball. There were never any ball games to go to, but now as an adult, I can understand why things were the way they were; as a man, I can understand what happened.

I do remember a few times when Dad and I did something together. There was the time when I was five or six and Dad took me fishing at the Power house below Nepco Lake. On the way, Dad took me back by Sailor's Rock to dig worms for bait. As we dug into the earth for wriggling red worms, I turned over a rock and a black salamander with white spots dart-ed out. Dad told me not to touch it because maybe it was poisonous. That was really good advice, thanks Dad. One time we took a trip to Grandpa John Born-bach's house to pick up a gigantic hog for slaughter.

We took it to a butchering place on the south end of Sherry, Wisconsin on Highway F. The plant was located on the west side of the road.

I really did love my dad when I was a young boy. I remember one summer evening when several of our family friends were having a picnic out by Lake Dexter. I must have been seven or eight years old, and I left the group of people by the picnic area. I wandered out toward the ditch by the highway waiting for Dad because he had to stay late after work. I knew it was going to be getting dark soon. I was worried Dad would get lost and not find us if he did not see me in the ditch.

As I was saying before, Dad and I really did not spend much time together. I saw him when he rushed through the kitchen door to eat supper each day at 3:40 and then I would see him when he came in for the night at seven or eight P.M. He was so worn out that he would fall asleep in his easy chair in front of the large bay window in the living room. When it was 9:00 P.M., Dad would get up, use the bathroom, and then go to bed. In the mornings, Dad would wake up at 5:30 A.M. and spend ten minutes on the throne in the bathroom; he would then head out to work for the day.

From what I gather, my parents had a few good years when they first started out. A divorce eventually came about when I was a teenager. I will not bring up details surrounding the circumstances of how the divorce took place. I myself am divorced after twenty five years of marriage, and, believe me, I know what emotional pain is. When I write about marriage or divorce, it is not to cast blame on anyone or to make them look bad. Divorce does leave scars and it leaves scar tissue. We think we are completely healed after time passes, but lurking deep below, hard feelings may still exist. For that reason, we may touch on the past but only briefly.

I do know that the relationship between my parents deteriorated as the years went on. Dad grew up with five brothers and three sisters. They were so poor that they could not pay attention. My grandfather John was an alcoholic who often left home for long periods of time, and no one would know where he went to. It was said that he worked in lumber camps somewhere, but Grandpa would not say where he went or what he did. I suspect that he worked around Bemidji in northern Minnesota. What we do know is that he drank up every penny that he earned.

When Grandpa was around, he was not always pleasant to be with. Once the drinking began, the abusive language would soon follow. Grandpa John's favorite place to drink was in the old stone tavern in Daul Town, which was built by the Drinkmann's in the 1880s. Once he drank himself into a stupor, he would wander back toward home and pass out somewhere on the way. Once he was found sleeping on Barry Reef's porch in Daul Town and another time he was found in a ditch along Oxbo Road. Grandpa

John drank so much that he racked up massive drinking debts with neighbors in the community. Dad and his brothers never had a real childhood as they were "farmed out." They worked for other farmers by the time they were eight or nine years old to pay off Grandpa's debts. I would imagine they picked stones and rocks from fields, baled hay, cleaned barns, drove tractors, and anything else that was required of them.

Meanwhile, back on the home farm, Grandma was cooking, cleaning, sewing, gardening, baking and raising chickens. Grandma worked twelve hours every Thursday baking, just to meet the needs of her nine children. She raised many chickens to get egg money to pay the bills. Once the laying hens became old, they were used to provide meat to put on the table. Grandma and her children ran the farm, and together, they put food on the table and clothes on their backs. Grandma was the glue which held her family together. Later, Grandma worked a job cleaning in the hospital in Cashfield to pay more of the bills.

Eventually, Grandpa came to his senses after Grandma threatened to leave him, and he began attending AA meetings. While Grandpa may have been abusive to his own family, he straightened up somewhat, and he was always nice to my sisters and me. Every time we came around, he showed interest in each one of us. He was always asking how we were doing in school; I really liked the old guy. Grandpa's favorite place to be was in his rocking chair by the window in the dining room. From there, he could look outside through the porch. Grandpa had arthritis, and on his window sill was some type of electrical con- traption which emitted voltage. The electrical shock would tingle through Grandpa's forearms and give him some measure of relief from the arthritis. Grand- pa was always wearing bib overalls, and Grandpa was quite a gross little pig. His favorite past time was chewing snuff while sitting in the rocker by the wood stove. Once he generated too much tobacco juice, he would spit it into the shirt cover of his overalls. Gross, gross, gross.

Grandma never did receive the love and at- tention from Grandpa which she so richly deserved. Grandpa was either too lazy to give it or he did not know how to show love. I do not know what drove Grandpa to drink and to become hooked on the de- mon of alcohol. One thing I do know is that his inade- quacy as a father was passed on to my father as Dad did not how to communicate love. My father, David, never really had a good role model to look towards for guidance as he was growing up. There was no "fa- ther figure" in his life to learn the good wholesome, nurturing qualities needed to become a good hus- band and father. I can only imagine how Dad's father treated him because I do not think the apple fell far from the tree. My siblings and I endured much as children at a young age. Beginning in the late 1960's we were wrapped on top of the center of the head by a large middle knuckle forcefully hitting down, or sometimes, we were squeezed around the neck by thumb and pointer finger by a man with powerful hands. There was also the name calling, names like sh*thead, pups... These are not names of love that one would call their children. This is not an example of nurturing or creating an environment of security for children to be raised in. I was told by Dad and his brothers that grandpa could get extremely mean. Grandpa would have been in danger of his sons beating him to death if anything ever happened to Grandma. I guess I knew how mean Grandpa might have been because sometimes that was how Dad acted. As an adult I found out what pushed dad into taking his frustrations out on his children. I honestly do not think that dad really knew how he was acting, when he was not nice to us.

Eventually, Mom left Dad. She ran around telling everyone that he was crazy. I guess that Dad really did not realize how bad things had become, but it took Mom leaving for him to come to his senses which lead him to a life changing experience with Jesus Christ. I inherited some of Dad's traits, and eventually, there was a day of reckoning for me also. I was faced with who I was and what I had become. People tell me that God does not exist, but I know better because God pulled me out of a pit which I had dug. A pit made by making wrong choices during my life growing up. In time, I, too, encountered Jesus and he made my life into something positive.

3

Chapter Three

Corn Flakes and Cold Tar

It was April of 1963, and I was three years old as I sat in a chair at the kitchen table in our upstairs apartment on South Street in Appaloosa. The sun was shining brilliantly through the kitchen window as I sat at the table eating my bowl of corn flakes. Today, we would go out into the country to see our new house that was being build east of Appaloosa on Strangeline Road. Strangeline Road was blacktopped for one mile as it ran southward down a hill on the dried up north branch of the seven mile, then further up another hill and then down a ways across the main channel of the Seven Mile Creek. This road and this creek had an indelible effect upon my life, and as I write this story fifty one years later, I feel a moving passion of affection for this area where I grew up.

In 1963, there were eleven dwellings on that one mile stretch of cold rolled black top. Beyond the creek was no a man's land that seemed like an infinite stretch of wilderness. In reality, a sandy fire lane stretched southward three more miles to the Ten Mile Creek.

We arrived at our new house and pulled onto the dirt driveway parking our 59 AMC Rambler in front of the garage. My parents went into the house to see how progress was coming along and to find out how soon it would be before we could move in. I, on the other hand, was more preoccupied with the sand left around the house from the excavation of the basement, so I decided to explore. It was afternoon, and as I went to the back of the house hugging the shadows, I crawled around in the cool sand. I noticed that not all of the sand was pushed up against the block walls, what was that sticky black stuff? The black tar was used to waterproof the cement block walls of the basement. Soon the rest of the sand would be pushed up against the house and then the lawn would be put in.

Our new $12,000 house was being built by a fella from Grand Rapids whose name was Larry Storch. Larry had recently built another house nearby which was fifty feet to the north. It was his dream to build an entire subdivision, but his dream was never realized as he died of a massive heart attack shortly upon the completion of our house.

Later, we went to the car and backed out of the driveway to make the trip back to our old house. As we left, we noticed the neighbor lady reaching into her mailbox to get the mail. We drove up to her, and as my parents introduced themselves to her, I could see that she had a fly swatter in her hand. The woman's name was Glenellen. As I looked out the window I saw a boy standing beside her. The boy was a few years older than me, and I could see that his mother was not very happy with him. It soon became apparent that the fly swatter in Glenellen's hand was not for swatting flies but rather for swatting boys. Glenellen swatted Roy across the side of his face, and in horror, I noticed a prominent red mark appear. In my mind I thought it was going to bleed. It was not until many years later that I realized that Roy was born with a birthmark where his mother had smacked him with the fly swatter.

I must say the Sweeny's were real characters, but then so was I. Even though the family only lived next to us for eight years, I am left with many memories. The Sweeny family consisted of the dad whose name was Klaus and his wife whose name of course was Glenellen. They had four children, Roy was the oldest and was three years older than me, then George who was two years older. Jean was my age, and Greg was three years younger than me. He was the same age as one of my sisters.

The Sweeny's did not have a garage at the time we moved onto Strangeline road, but they did have a sandbox where the future garage would eventually be built. As Greg played in the sand box, he would eat sand and their dog Brownie would usually run nearby. One evening at suppertime my sister Glenda was near the sandbox as Greg played. As she reached out to pet the dog, it bit her. Klaus immediately took the dog out back and shot it.

It seems dogs were an endangered species at the Sweeny house. I remember a time when Roy was twelve or thirteen. At that time, he had a rather dangerous hobby. He would shoot arrows straight up into the air in their backyard to see just how high he could make them go. Keep in mind that an arrow eventually has to come back down and those arrows could have fallen back onto the roof of their house, or worse yet, they could have come down in our yard and killed one of my sisters or me. On one particular day, Roy was shooting arrows into the air, and as one came down, it killed their dog Laddie as he stood by the garden.

I remember another incident with Roy and animals. Roy was near the back end of a horse one evening as it was walking down Strangeline Road. I do not know what Roy did, but the horse ended up kicking him in the head. Everyone in our neighborhood was scared that night wondering if Roy was going to die. As it turns out, Roy did survive after a metal plate was put in his head. I am amused as I remember these stories because Glenellen once remarked to my mother that she thought I was mentally retarded. Perhaps she really meant one of her children?

Another incident involved Greg, his older brother George, and me. Greg outweighed me by thirty pounds, so I really had a difficult time getting the best of him when we wrestled. One particular day we were wrestling around outside the north end of the Sweeny house by their propane tank. I was getting the best of Greg so he started crying. Well, George heard Greg so he came after me to beat the crap out of me. I took off running for the woods, circled around, and came back across our garden. I could see George was starting to catch up to me, so I quickly picked up a rock flung it and dropped him in the garden.

There was one humorous memory I have of Mrs. Sweeny. From our house, we could see Glenellen as she bent over and weeded her onions in their garden on hot summer days. Glenellen was not what you would call thin, and on one particular day my mother happened to be looking out back through our kitchen window. She soon exclaimed "that's quite a view Glenellens giving us from her garden." Glenellen was originally from Wantowalk down on the south line of Juneau County. One weekend, her brother Omar came up to visit with their family and was he ever a story teller. Usually when men flex their biceps the muscle bulges up a bit, but in Omar's case it dropped down. This was supposedly because he once tore his arm on a nail out in the barn. Like I said, Omar was a story teller.

I wrote earlier about playing Daniel Boone and our building of forts out in the woods. One summer, Klaus came home with a load of barn boards or rough cut lumber, and many of them were one by twelves. Those boards made the most magnificent fort in

Sweeny's back yard. Over the years, Greg became a first rate home builder. The handiwork of his company, G & G builders, can be found on many fine properties up and down the Petenwell flowage in Juneau County, Wisconsin.

Dirks Bentley, Roger Martin, and Klaus Sweeny had their country band called the good Ole Boys, and I can remember how their music wafted through the neighborhood on many a hot summer night. I will never get the song, "I've Got a Tiger by the Tail," by Buck Owens out of my mind. The neighbor boys also became good musicians in their own right. I think Roy Sweeny may have played guitar and his brother George played drums. Another boy by the name of Duane Allman played guitar and, later, steel guitar. I remember one night the boys were practicing. I walked up to them and asked, "What does this do?" Before they could answer, I flipped a switch on their amp and there was a loud pop. I never heard any more music the rest of the night.

I think the Sweeny's moved away in 1971 when they ended up buying an old farm house west of Appaloosa with eighty acres, a barn, and some out buildings; it was a beautiful area. Duane Allman relayed a story one time from when he went to visit the Sweeny boys after they moved out to the farm. Klaus happened to be grilling hamburgers and Greg was eating them just as fast as he could grill them. When Glenellen saw how many hamburgers were missing, she said, "Klaus, ain't that cute, Greg just ate five hamburgers."

Looking back, I remember so many fond memories such as walking out in the woods while Greg rode his cast iron tractor. In the mornings, we would pass the red ant hill while meandering through the hazel nut brush. In the field nearby, we would visit our little friend, a baby red fox living in the brush pile.

Steven Bornbach

Steven Bornbach

4

Chapter Four

Roles People Play in Our Development.

There have been some very important people in the course of my life, relatives, neighbors, and others. I cannot emphasize enough just how important each of them were to me, not only in the past, but also today. One such person who was very important is a man who I'll call XMan. XMan is shy and extremely conscious of being in the spotlight, so I need to be sensitive and exercise as much tact as I possibly can. There is no way I can skip XMan in my autobiography, even though some people will undoubtedly know who I am writing about. For everyone else, let's just pretend this person was a very valuable witness in a mob trial and that his identity must be kept secret, as he is in a witness protection program.

Our house was completed in 1963 while my dad had been working in the paper mill. So when XMan completed his service to our country and returned to Wisconsin, he was later invited by my father to put his application in at Appaloosa Papers. It was no surprise that he was hired by the mill. Once he was hired, Dad invited him to come and stay with us. XMan soon became my roommate, and he stayed a very long time. He became a member of the family and made many contributions over the years. XMan soon remodeled our kitchen, put in a bedroom downstairs, put in a well in the back yard, drove us to church every week, went with us on every vacation, and even went with us every time we visited relatives. It was not long before XMan decided to stay permanently with us as he purchased the lot next door and then built a garage upon it. He continued on as my roommate for the next several years until I left home.

I was very appreciative of XMan for the attention which he gave me upon his initial arrival to our house. He gave me my first 15 pound bow with arrows when I was eight, and then he bought me a Shark thirty five pound long bow when I turned twelve. XMan took me to Antler Archers for shooting contests which he participated in, and he took me to J & K Archery to hang out with friends that he worked with.

XMan was extremely intelligent and he built our first color TV from a kit in 1967; he also made a radio out of a Heath kit. Unfortunately as a child, I was never a genius, nor was I capable of keeping an attention span for very long. When I was seven or eight, I was taught to shoot a bow and the arrows, but I just wanted to have fun; I did not want to be a perfectionist. When XMan bought a mini bike, I wanted to ride it, but I did not want to fix it. Oh, I guess I did want to fix it, but I just could not grasp how to. I am the kind of person that needs to see how to do something, hear how to do something, and I need hands on experience with someone walking me through the process. XMan was a perfectionist and I was not, so we drifted apart. To make matters worse, we did not have the same type of personality so I could not understand him and he could not understand me. XMan loved to eat everything, but I was a picky eater and this created many more problems. So many times I was called slooky, I was told to go to bed hungry if I did not like what everyone else was eating, I was told to "use my head." I was called stupid kid, dumb kid, and the list goes on. I remember trying to build a boat from a Boy Scout book. It was a simple wooden cut out with a rubber band for a propeller. The remark I was given by XMan was "that is not how you do it," but he never worked with me to show me the right way. As a teenager, XMan and I drifted so far apart that our relationship never became what it could have been.

1967 was a year of endings for me when it came to having any type of personal relationships with male role models in our home. The semi - personal relationship with XMan faded from my life. At the same time, the limited access that I had with my father also disappeared due to emotionally traumatizing scenes that he had recently witnessed. For me, life would never be the same, and I would look to other men in the neighborhood for acceptance. As an adult, I am now able to look back on the circumstances that surrounded the past; as an adult, I now understand why Dad acted as he did. The last event I remember Dad and I doing together as a father and son took place in a woods west of Prince Edwards. A friend of the family by the name of Roy Elmhorst was going to build a house on a hill overlooking Moccasin creek. He asked my dad to dig a basement for the new house, so my dad borrowed his father's green John Deere crawler. The large trees had been cut down but the stumps needed a little extra persuasion to release themselves from the tight earth. Dad began boring holes under the stumps and then packed in a stick or two of dynamite. He looked at me and told me to run away as fast as I could as he began lighting the dynamite fuse. I had just reached a tree and I peered out from behind it to see dad running wildly toward me with a huge grin on his face. Seconds later a thundering kaboom permeated the stillness around us. Chunks of wood then began falling from the sky. Afterwards, Dad strolled back to the mean green digging machine to finish digging the basement and I played down below in the creek.

When I was entering my teenage years, Mom began working outside the home and since that time we have not been close either. I was having problems at school from day one and it seems like I really did not have anyone to talk to. I became a loner, ready to latch on to anyone who would be my friend. This would eventually set the stage for the dark years of my teenage life.

Gust front "shelf cloud" (or "arcus") on the leading edge of a derecho-producing convective system. The photo was taken by Brittney Misialek (Courtesy of Brittney Misialek).

On a hot summer day in 1967, XMan drove mom, my siblings and me to Fleet Farm in Cashfield, but we never made it. We hopped in the old Ford sedan and began our trip; however, when we were three or four miles southeast of Cashfield a violent storm came upon us. As we proceeded west on Highway 10 an ominous looking shelf cloud appeared from the west and overtook us. It filled the entire horizon of the western sky. Shelf clouds often are at the front of a squall line of ferocious storms capable of producing winds over one hundred miles per hour. This shelf cloud was indeed dangerous and extremely violent, as a matter of fact, Mom would probably be dead if it were not for XMan keeping her in the car. What happened was as we were driving down the road, the wind picked up. The wind was so strong that the car slowed to a stop. We could not go forward. The wind kept blowing under the car, and as it did, we could feel ourselves being lifted up. Let me tell you, the Hail Mary's were just a flying as Mom tried to open up the passenger door to go into the ditch, but she could not get the door open. It was just as well because any wind strong enough to lift a car would have just as surely been able to pick up a human being and blow them into the next county. Eventually, the wind subsided and we turned the car around to go back home. As we headed south on Highway K, we saw a trailer house demolished with the toilet and bathtub lying by the road. On our left, we saw where straight line winds had pulled many large oaks and maples out of the heavy clay soil. The fury of that storm was incredible and the wind speed must have been 80 – 100 miles per hour.

It is quite remarkable the influence environment, relatives, neighbors, church, classmates, teachers, and daily events have on a child while they are growing up. Few if any of my neighbors have any clue as to how important they were to me as a child; those same people are still important to me today. There were a couple of other families in our neighborhood that I could mention; however, they were not people who impacted my life. Lester Smart, the Sweeny's, Coburn's, Flintstone's, Picken's, Sculley's, Allman's, and Smedstead's all had and still have a major place in my memories, not only of the distant past but also in the recent past. People may be able to take your possessions; disease, age and accidents may take your loved ones; evil people may take your life, but no one can take your memories.

The Flintstones were our neighbors who lived across the road from us. I will try and share a few tidbits of Flintstone family history, and hopefully, I will not deviate too far from the facts. Donald Flintstone grew up in a sod house on a prairie in the region of Lynch, Nebraska. Donald's mother had been a teacher at a one room school house and that is where she met Donald's father. After they married, it was decided they would settle in an area west of Appaloosa, Wisconsin. The area of land Donald's dad bought was sometimes called Mentone by the old timers. A railroad ran just north of the intersection of present day highways GG and 173, and it was that spot where the old steam locomotives would stop to take on water.

World War Two arrived upon the world and Donald, being patriotic as he was, became involved with the Army and Air Force as a machinist mechanic. Traveling with the military gave young men opportunities for recreation during off times and that is how Donald found his bride to be. A young gal by the name of Lily, whose maiden name was White, grew up in the vicinity of New Britain, Connecticut. Donald was stationed in that area during WWII and one day the service men were lined up to go roller skating. Lilly happened to be at the skating rink and as she noticed Donald, she remarked to her mother, "I'm gonna marry that man," and the rest became history.

After the war, Donald and Lilly located to Strangeline Road where they lived for many years. He became a machinist at the Appaloosa Edwards paper mill in Prince Edwards. Lilly found employment with Foodland West in Grand Rapids. They were a friendly and kind couple who truly loved others. Our young family located to their neighborhood many years later and we were made to feel welcome by many random acts of kindness. Lilly used to bring us expired twinkies, Ho Hos and frosted cupcakes from the store, and Donald would let me play horse with him out behind his garage. I can still hear him say "allie oop" as he would make lay ups and hook shots. Donald was also an incredible hunter and fisherman, I do not think he ever came home empty handed. I remember one day when Donald took me rabbit hunting in the Seven Mile Creek bottoms, it was below zero and I was so cold. Donald was not wearing any gloves, but he offered to warm me up. As I put my hands in his, it was like sticking my hands into a warm blanket.

Donald and Lily were several years older than my mom and dad. My dad and mom in turn were a few years older than Donald and Lilly's teenage kids whose names were Fred, Barney, Wilma, and Bety. One of my first memories of Fred Flintstone was when I was staring out of our bay window in the living room and watching Fred smoke the tires off of his car. The vehicle may have been a Chevelle, but one thing I am sure of is that no one could see across the road because the smoke from the tires was too thick. When I was a teenager, Fred would have me come over to his house on Church Avenue to pile his firewood. I can still see him smoking his cigarette in the kitchen as he would ask me if "I would like a pop."

Wilma Flintstone was my baby sitter for a time until she graduated from high school and married Luke Skywalker. It was on November 13, 1965 that I was a ring bearer for their wedding at United Church of Christ by the bridge in Appaloosa. Luke's little sister, Leia, was the flower girl. There was a reception for the soon to be newlyweds the night before the wedding at the Bender Corral just over the viaduct on Highway 13, west of Grand Rapids. I can still remember eating the mashed potatoes, gravy and baked chicken, mmmmmmmmmmm.

Barney had been in the Air Force, and upon

completion to the service he entered the Prince Edwards paper mill. Barney married a woman by the name of Patrice, and they had a daughter by the name of Pebbles. It was at this time in the early 70s that my mother babysat for them at our house, before she was employed outside the home. I remember Barney lived on Deer Ridge Road at the time and he used to drive what I think was a dark gray or black Olds Cuttlass. One day Barney took me to his house and introduced me to one of his favorite songs called "InaGodDadavida" by Iron Butterfly. What a long song that turned out to be. Barney was an avid photographer who apparently was athletic because one day he took me to the top of Castle Rock by Necedah and photographed me. I was so nervous to be up that high in the air. There were also times that Barney took me fishing on the Wisconsin River by Fourteen Mile Creek and where the Ten Mile flows into the river. When a northern was about to take the bait, Barney's advice was to "take your time and smoke a cigarette while the northern swallows the minnow." Barney and his family are partly responsible for my work ethic today. They let me burn their garbage, feed Dino their dog, rake their lawn, and shear their shrubs. I am thankful that Donald, Lilly, and their kids were such wonderful people to grow up with.

5

Chapter Five

Elementary and Grade School

In life, it is not the destination that matters most but rather the journey to get there. Twelve years of my life were spent with the Appaloosa class of '78. There were good times and there were bad times, but we were together, going through life with one another from childhood into adulthood. The Appaloosa school system, our common bond, is where we met each day of the school year. Each day was a building block in the mosaic of our lives and each classmate was a thread of that mosaic, weaved through my life. Some colors signify good experiences by their bright cheery hues while other colors seem drab and lifeless emphasizing turbulence and struggles. Many classmates were quite comical all the way through school, such as Gary and Barry who used to have fish swallowing contests in the high school commons.

We started out in innocence when elementary school first began, but that innocence evaporated over the years with the start of the Vietnam War. No, we did not fight the war ourselves, but we were a part of it from kindergarten all the way through our freshman year of high school. Day after day the war was brought into our homes with the evening news on television, and it was very much a part of our lives as we studied current events in school. Unfortunately, life is not perfect and neither were we as we grew up in the best of times and the worst of times. The assassination of John F. Kennedy, his brother Robert and Rev. Martin Luther King Jr., along with the Kent State shootings, were a reflection of what our turbulent society at its worst could be like. Human behavior stinks when people sink to animalistic actions.

Elementary school is where it all began in 1965. There were three kindergarten teachers, Mrs. Lettuce, Mrs. Cane, and Mrs. Cowbell. My teacher at the time was Mrs. Lettuce.

Just down the hallway from our room was the playground. Upon going through the hallway doors and exiting out onto the playground, one would be greeted by the following sights: a large tree was on the left with the blacktop cut out around the perimeter in a circular fashion. When it would rain, the cut out part would fill up with water forming a moat. To the southwest were the slide, swings, and the monkey bars (many a child fell and broke their arms over the years on those monkey bars). In back of the playground equipment was a sledding hill and to the north a field for playing sports.

Our kindergarten consisted of half days. Activities learned or reinforced were shoe tying, ABC's, numbers, hygiene and lots of craft projects. For those who were good, there was milk and cookies during rest period and sometimes there was the special treat of chocolate milk. In Mrs. Lettuce's class, some of us would miss out on those treats as we were spending quality time alone behind the piano. Actually, we were being punished for transgressions, such as not being able to tie our shoes good enough. Kindergarten was quite educational as we learned how to make butter with milk cream and beaters. There were also field trips to the old fire station under the water tower by the bridge. On another field trip, we went to the Berg farm on Lynn Hill Road where we were taken on a hay ride through the woods along a stream; another trip took us out to the Joslin museum on Ten Mile Avenue.

In first grade, there were two teachers, Mrs. MacIntosh and Mrs. Sledge. My teacher was Mrs. Sledge. She introduced several of us boys to Mr. Sylvester her ruler. Brian, Gary and I regularly had our hands laid out upon the teacher's desk, as Sylvester the ruler would be brought down hard upon our knuckles. Infractions such as saying "hecky darn" and other such petty crimes were the reason for those wonderful times of corporal punishment.

Two teachers taught second grade. They were Mrs. Gristmill and Mrs. Korn. Mrs. Korn was a great lady who was always understanding. She always looked for the good in children. Mrs. Korn and I attended the same church, and as an adult, we have had many informational conversations. I found out from her that she could sense that there were struggles in my life due to problems at home and on the playground. Out of eight teachers in elementary school, that teacher was one of the four who seemed to care the most about me. Our second grade assignments were often challenging. One such assignment was to memorize the 21 line poem "Hiawatha" by Henry Wadsworth Longfellow. I am not sure if there were other stanzas or not, but the opening lines began with, "By the shores of Gitchee Gumee, by the shining big sea water..."

We had a real interesting fellow in our class by the name of Howard Juxton. Somehow he earned the name screwy Howard. Howard always told a lot of tall tales, and he could always be counted on to entertain our class with ring worm, poison ivy, and a host of other maladies. As an adult, Howard joined the National Guard. One day he was in his mother's kitchen showing her his revolver when it went off and killed him, he died in his mother's arms.

Our gym teacher in elementary school was Mrs. Newt. Mrs. Newt taught us how to square dance, play Captain May I, Red Light – Green Light, Elimination, Simon Says, Pom Pom Poloway, and a host of other activities. Mrs. Wenzel was our school librarian, and she made reading fun as she would read chapters from story books to us during the week. My all-time favorite book from which she read was, "The Boxcar Children." Our music teacher was Mrs. Green.

She was the key person who trained us to perform for seasonal music programs that were held in the gym. One program comes to mind from third grade in which Randy, Brian, and I formed a trio as we sang a song about the moon. Mrs. Green would periodically look to me and say, "Do not lift your head so high when you sing."

When I was in third grade, the teachers were Mrs. Cough and Mrs. Korn. Mrs. Korn had moved up a grade that year with us. Both third grade classes were held in the annex out by the athletic field. The annex building is currently being used for administration offices. Mrs. Cough happened to be my teacher, and she was fresh out of college. It was obvious that teachers were not yet taught how to observe signs of ADD or ADHD among children. For some reason I drove this teacher to the point of exasperation, so often I found myself in the hallway getting my hair pulled, and listening to Mrs. Cough yell into my face. Too bad Mrs. Korn was teaching across the hallway so I could not have access to her.

Fourth grade was our final class in elementary school as we finished up in the spring of 1970. Periodically, we would go in back of the school to play by the swamp and look for tad poles, frogs, and garter snakes. Quite often, the boys would be in the principal's office writing one hundred times, "I will not go out to the swamp." One historical event was taking place each day as we attended third and fourth grade; that was construction of the new senior high school, which held its first class in the fall of 1970. Many years later our class would be the fifth class to attend the new facilities. Observant young souls looking west from the annex windows could see daily a large crane lifting large steel girders for the school roof. Just over the hill and behind the trees, a silhouette of the tall steel crane sections would reach up into the sky as it peered over the tree line.

When fourth grade arrived, we no longer had just one teacher. Rather, there was the home room teacher and then other teachers who specifically taught math, science, and language. Mrs. Henry taught language and art; Mrs. Caan taught reading (In Mrs. Caan's class, we memorized and learned to sing "The Star Spangled Banner"); Mrs. Sneip taught spelling and penmanship; Mr. Lennon taught science and arithmetic. In Mr. Lennon's class, we learned to multiply and divide.

I just cannot figure out why teachers from my elementary school years were so violent. There must not have been psychology courses for teachers to take in college before being hired for teaching assignments in the public schools. Either that, or corporal punishment was the preferred method for teachers in dealing with children... Mr. Lennon may have known a lot about science and math "but his treatment of students was brutish." I remember wanting so badly to learn in Mr. Lennon's class, so I studied hard. In class, Mr. Lennon would have students raise their hands, and he would then call on one of them to give the answer out loud. I do not know if I volunteered answers too frequently or if the guy just did not like me because he did not call on me. I would hold my arm up waiting and waiting to be called upon but it never happened. Eventually, I just blurted out the answers, so after class he would march me to the sink in back of the class room. There he would grab me by the neck and continue squeezing until he felt a measure of satisfaction. There were other inappropriate behaviors which took place in that classroom when Mr. Lennon made examples of children who he did not like. Mr. Lennon called me big mouth Bornbach because I began blurting out the answers. Eventually, I became discouraged and my math scores suffered. When other boys like Jim, Craig, and Keith started getting lower test scores, Mr. Lennon would make an example of all four of us by calling us the "F club." I feel it is important to remember that children will one day become adults. All throughout childhood and adolescence they are being molded by teachers and people in authority. How we treat others often determines whether others will sink or swim. I began making poor choices by the time I became an adolescent, and mother wondered why. It is interesting to note that each boy in the "F club" went on to become dope heads.

In closing the chapter on my elementary school memories, I would be remiss if the cafeteria were not mentioned. I was part of the cold lunch crowd since I was such a fussy eater. We sat in the first three rows of tables along the far wall, across from the doors where you enter for the hot lunch line. Sitting together at those long tables in the twilight of elementary school innocence, we spent many lunch hours speculating as to whether or not Santa Clause really existed.

The middle school used to be a high school before the new school was built. The old building was constructed sometime around 1917, about the time of WWI. Upon entering the school from the front entry, a visitor would see the receptionist's and principal's office immediately on the left. Across the hall from there would be Mrs. Haza's classroom. Straight ahead from the entry would be the steps leading up to study hall and the library. On the first floor and over to the right would be the fifth grade classrooms. Mrs. Seatbelt's room was in the southeast corner of the building. The two story structure ran along First Street and then wrapped around to an older part of the structure on the east side, which contained a small gym where the girls had their physical activities. The boys, on the other hand, used the larger gym under the supervision of Physical Education instructor Liam Olds.

One of the favorite games the boys played was long base, where a kicker stood at home plate and kicked a ball to open spaces throughout the gym. The rest of the gym was an "outfield," where opposing team members could catch the kicker's ball to make an out. The object of the game was to run the length of the gym to a "safe" mat hanging from the wall on the other end of the gym and then back to home plate without getting out. The game was sort of like running a gauntlet. In the outfield, anyone who obtained the kicked ball had the opportunity to throw the ball at any one of the runners going to and from the mat to get them out; it was quite exhilarating to be one of the runners and to fight for survival to stay-alive in the game.

There was a boy in our class who was bigger and stronger than everyone else. His name was Tom. Tom was very good natured and was never mean to anyone; by the age of 14, Tom could control the longbase ball with his finger tips on one hand, and he could throw the ball like a rocket. One thing I remember about Tom was his love for Star Trek and the show "The F.B.I." Tom had extremely large knuckles and that was because he would get excited while watching his favorite television shows and then would punch the floor with his fists. Tom died in an automobile accident on Highway 33 by the bridge in Carthage, Wisconsin around 1990 or 1991 on his return from Summer Fest in Milwaukee. He would have been around thirty one years old at the time.

Our principle in fifth grade was Mr. Fonzlie and our teachers were Mrs. Jennings– spelling and science; Mrs. Fuser – writing, English, and art; and Mrs. Haza – reading, math, and social studies. Mrs. Haza also taught us frontier history along with the fifty states and their capitals. Do you the reader ever remember memorizing all fifty of our United States and their capitals? Sometime during that year Mrs. Fuser married and she was then called Mrs. Seatbelt. It was in her room that we watched the spacecraft missions to the moon and their entry into earth's orbit before they would have their splashdown. Who can forget news commentators Roger Mudd and Walter Cronkite? Fifth grade was quiet as we were the youngest class in school that year. Each of our fifth grade teachers had an amiable personality and a desire to teach. I am grateful for each of them.

Sixth grade was in the south west area of the school on the first floor and the teachers were Mr. Leonard Nimoy – writing, English, and art; Miss Hershey – reading and spelling; Mr. Albert Einstein – math, social studies, and, Mrs. Pilsen – science and health. In Mrs. Pilsen's class, we learned of her passion for snakes. We also read many good books. The one I remember most is "Old Yeller." I believe Mrs. Pilsen died of brain cancer not long after she taught our class.

Each of our sixth grade teachers were most helpful and none of the women inflicted any physical pain upon us. The men on the other hand still displayed the old German philosophy of corporal punishment. If you woke Mr. Nimoy up from napping behind his desk, you ran the risk of getting choked. I think the most anger I ever saw displayed by any teacher was by Mr. Einstein. Mr. Einstein loved to tell stories of his life and personal philosophies, and while he could be quite cordial, he often erupted into a violent temper. When angered, he would pound his fists upon his desk as his face turned red. Any student who was the target of his wrath would be made to kneel in front of the windows on the hard wooden floor until class was dismissed. Mr. Einstein was totally against seat belt use in motor vehicles because his brother was killed in an accident while driving a truck and was unable to escape from a truck fire.

Incidentally, our principle in sixth grade was Mr. Gale Gordon; he was very tough and gruff. I do not know if anyone remembers the "I love Lucy" show, but Mr. Gordon was very much like the show character Fred Mertz. Rumor had it that Mr. Gordon was a boxer in his younger days. One day, a big old bully by the name of Gary Collins became belligerent in the principal's office. Gary took a swing at Mr. Gordon but ended up on the floor, and that is where he stayed until the police arrived.

Mr. Nimoy was my sixth grade home room teacher. In that class, Mike Fredrickson sat in front of me. Mike's favorite past time would be to continually scratch his head over his desk until he built up a pile of dandruff to gross everyone out. Strange things happened when Mr. Nimoy would fall asleep. One day Tom Terrific stapled his fingers together. Just how do you go about stapling your fingers together? I never figured that out.

During sixth grade and going into seventh, new kids would arrive while others would leave. Sherri left due to the tragedy of the death of her mother, while Mark and his brother Todd moved to Michigan somewhere. They eventually moved back to the area and attended Lincoln High School in Grand Rapids. Their family grew up dirt poor, but each of them turned out to be good business men. One has a trucking business for selling produce, another was involved with a mall, and the other brothers have an R.V business and exhaust shop. One new arrival to our class that year was John. John was an architect's son. His father designed many buildings for elderly and low income housing on Section and Cedar Streets in Appaloosa. John was a very quiet person and after a year as our classmate he left. It was rumored that he had been sent to a military academy school by his father.

Our seventh grade teachers were Mr. Lithgow – civics, Mr. Swisher – math, Mrs. Yeller – reading, and Miss Macon – science. Mr. Gordon was still our principle. Miss. Macon married the next year and became Mrs. Lime. Miss Macons's room was on the south side on the second floor and just before Mr. Eastheads's room to the west. Her window ledge was always full of plants, cocoons, and all types of interesting bugs and other fascinating objects. We learned about all types of creatures from the smallest to the largest as we studied amoebas, mollusks, invertebrates and vertebrates, and bacteria in petri dishes. Learning in that class was so much fun. We were given the most awesome opportunities to really learn about the wonders of our world. Miss Macon had a frequent saying each day which was, "If I hear any-body say ugly, they will get an F for the day." This was one class where girls received more F's than the boys. As jars of small snakes and big hairy spiders were passed around the room, girls would say, "Ooh, that's ugly," and a voice would immediately ring out saying, "That's an F!"

In seventh grade a Native American family attended our school. Of course, they were not the first, but the Holcomb's made their presence known as they enjoyed making trouble. The brothers often assembled destructive blow darts made from Bic pens and needles which when blown, would stick deep into the oak doors of the bathrooms. I remember Art Kastenschmidt's warehouse on North Young Street was burglarized by the brothers three times in the 70's and 80's. There were also the times that Dodger Holcomb kept looking over my shoulder in the gym locker room until he was able to get the combination of my lock. I received a brand new Car-avel watch for Christmas one year, and then one day it mysteriously disappeared from my locker. I was of slender build but Dodger was more solid. His man-nerisms were often intimidating, so I was afraid to ask for my watch back. Now Dodger was a conniver who was always ready to run a scam for money. This was evidenced by what happened the very first day of school when I met him in Mr. Einstein's class. I took an interest in Dodger that morning, so before class started, I asked him what tribe he belonged to. Dodger's response was that it would cost me a dollar to find out. One day there was a crowd of kids gathered around two boys who were about to engage in a fist fight. One of the boys was Dodger Holcomb and the other was Mark Kenmore. Mark Kenmore was your average clean cut American boy, quiet, smart, respectful, and caring. Mark was also very athletic and was involved in many sports all throughout school. It is no surprise that he won many boxing matches later in life when he was assigned to a ship in the Navy. So here we have a crowd of kids yelling while Mark and Dodger are in a fighting stance, circling each other and waiting for the other fighter to throw a punch. I weaseled my way up to the fighters and shouted, "Hit him Mark!" Apparently, I was too close to the action because Dodger immediately turned around and punched me hard in the mouth. My lip split open with blood spattering everywhere, so I ran towards the school to go into the bathroom for cold wet toweling to stop the bleeding. Mark caught up to me on the sidewalk to see if I was all right and I told him I was ok. I then handed Mark a nickel to go back and punch Dodger for me, but he never did.

On the playground, kids were always kicking red rubber balls onto the roof in the warm weather. In the winter there were huge snow piles pushed to the east onto the tennis court and up against the fence. It was on those piles that each boy's manhood, or lack thereof, was established as the game "King of the Hill" was played every day at recess.

Two women teachers of the "arts" really stand out in my mind. Both ladies were quiet, and every student really liked them. Miss Hubba was an art teacher who made art class extremely fun as she played records on her phonograph while moving around and instructing students as they created their projects. One of our favorite record albums was by Three Dog Night, and the most requested song was "Jeremiah Was a Bullfrog." Mrs. Mulligan was the other outstanding teacher who kept us in tune with the times as we had to know the top ten hits of the weekly top ten music chart from the radio. Songs we learned and sang were "He's a Real No Where Man" and "Yesterday" by the Beatles, "Bridge over Troubled Waters" by Simon and Garfunkel, "You're so vain" by Carly Simon. Of course we also sang folk songs such as, "This Land is Your Land", "If I Had a Hammer", and "The ballad of John Tuttle."

As a student, I did not really stand out. I was just average and ordinary, so it is with great fondness that I remember something that I was somewhat good at, forensics. In both seventh and eighth grade, I took part in a play with several other students. The name of the play was called, "The Incredible Cookie Caper." The first year we performed the play was outstanding, but the second year we performed it mediocre. Why was the first year so much better? Well I suppose it had something to do with Bonnie Raitt being part of the cast. Bonnie was very outgoing and charismatic. Her artistic abilities in acting and art transcended to greater heights later in high school.

73

Sixteen out of thirty three Appaloosa Junior High School students earned forensic contest honors in 1973. That year we advanced to the forensics competition at P.J. Jacobs Junior High School in Stevens Point. I honestly do not remember how we placed in the Point competition, but looking back, I am proud of having participated in those events.

Eighth grade quickly arrived and with it a new batch of teachers, all of whom I liked. Mr. Easthead taught science, Mr. Newman – math, Mr. Williams – geography, Miss Celery – English, Mrs. Bean – music, and Mr. Goodrich – industrial arts. The most memorable teacher for all of the boys had to be Mr. Goodrich who was a crusty old former marine. His body was afflicted with rheumatoid arthritis, but he compensated for his joint pain with erasers. With deadly precision he would zero in on a head shot for any student who was not paying attention while he was teaching. Another favorite punishment Mr. Goodrich meted out was to make students stand up close to the blackboard on their tip toes. He would draw a circle on the blackboard once he found out where their nose touched and make them stand in that position for a considerable amount of time. If the flying erasers did not set us straight, then the blackboard would. Mr. Goodrich acted tough and he was tough; however, he had a heart of gold and really loved kids. His was the art of tough love.

6

Chapter Six

Fire and Water

Dad decided to take a ride into Appaloosa late one summer day in 1967, and the purpose of the trip was to pick up a washer and dryer set from Keefer's on Vilas avenue in Appaloosa. My sister Fran and I went along for the ride. When Dad began loading the appliances, I decided to walk around to the back of the garage. Fran said she noticed a dog tied up, and sure enough, a little black and white chijuajua was standing by the back porch breezeway. I am not certain what happened next because Fran went to pet the dog and it liked her but when I went to pet the dog it bit me. Knowing my squirrely, impulsive behavior, I probably teased the dog, or maybe, I went to pet the dog but saw that it did not like me so I turned to run away.

One thing is for sure, as I turned to run, the dog caught me before he could reach the end of his chain. Suddenly, I felt a tearing sensation in the lower calf of my left leg. When I looked down, I saw a hole in the skin the size of my thumb with flesh protruding through it. It became obvious that we had to get to a doctor right away. On the way, Dad was furious.

I remember he said the following words through gritted teeth, "When we get home, you're going to get it." I always wondered, what was his problem anyway, the dog bite was no skin off his leg. Perhaps Dad was angry that his son acted up at another person's house so he was embarrassed, or perhaps, he was worried about an unforeseen medical bill. Whatever the reason, Dad's attitude soon changed once we entered the doctor's office.

Doctor Pfeiffer met us at the Appaloosa Medical Center. He soon arrived with syringes and needles filled with some type of medication to give me shots. Due to the trauma, I just cannot remember how many shots there were or where I received them. Dad and the doctor were trying their hardest to keep my mind preoccupied with thoughts other than those shots. For a while, I was laughing and crying at the same time, and before long, Fran and I were on our way home, each with a lollipop.

I had built a fort with leftover scraps that my friend gave me and I went to that fort at edge of the woods the day after the dog bit me. I remember it was an oppressively hot day as I stood alongside my refuge eating my jelly sandwich loaded with butter. There was no breeze and the air was stagnant. There was no sound but that of insects. One sound in particular caught my attention, a loud buzzing interspersed with rhythmical ticks. Looking into the hazelnut brush I noticed a bug, long and black with large webbed wings. It was a Cicada. I was lost in thought over the exotic creature when I felt something wet on the back of my leg. Looking down I wondered how melted butter and strawberry jelly could have landed there. In horror, I realized then the mess was not from my sandwich. It was blood and pus.

We were used to having vehicles fly over the top of the hill where the Pickins family lived. Many of the young bucks from Saratoga flew north down the cold rolled blacktop of Strangeline Road from Hardpressed Avenue. Local travelers had to endure three miles of dirt fire lanes before coming to the paved road on the south side of Seven Mile Creek by Brown's house. From there, drivers would put their pedals to the metal. By the time they passed our house they were doing seventy or eighty miles per hour. One day as I sat on our front steps I noticed something oddly different, a go cart traveling down the road, then another, and another. Now, I was not certain of who these people were or what they were doing on the other side of the hill between our house and Sculleys, but Gregg Allman Jr. said they were folks from Tennessee who were working on a pipeline for the local paper mill. Since they talked funny and were from Tennesee, I thought maybe they were hillbillies. After all, the Beverly Hillbillies were from Tennessee, you know, Grannie, Uncle Jed, Jethro, and Ellie May.

Well this group of people were real friendly. They must have temporarily bought the land on the other side of the hill as it was not long before there were a half dozen cement pads poured for all of the trailers to sit on. The next item of business for them was to erect a six stall garage to work on the go carts and their other mechanical toys. Their driveway consisted of a two tenth of a mile oval race track upon which they raced their go carts. By the next summer, the pipeline was completed and our southern friends left the area to find employment elsewhere. For a time, I had the gravel racetrack all to myself, and that is where I began riding XMan's Yamaha 80 motorcycle.

In 1971, Sweeny's moved away from the house next door to us. Arthur and Mary Shaw were the next occupants of the house before moving west to Hollywood Road. Roger and Deb Gerzmehle were the next residents until an opportunity arose for them to purchase the house that Roger grew up in on Point Basse, in Appaloosa. The Coburns moved in after the Gerzmehle's left. James and Paula Coburn seemed nice enough with their three boys, John, Paul and Ringo. John was the same age as one of my siblings, but Paul and Ringo were a year or two younger. James grew up in the area of Coon Valley, Wisconsin and he decided to move onto Strangeline Road upon finding employment with a local public utility. James became a lineman and many years later became manager of the same public utility.

When I first met James, he was a real tough guy who liked to show all of his martial arts and self-defense tactics on me. James had been in Vietnam. I do not remember what his assignment was, but it really must have been hard core. I think he spoke fluent Thai. I could be wrong, but he was fluent in one of those eastern languages. The moves he used on me were something that Rambo would have used in the movie "First Blood" with Sylvester Stalone. James was also a master at games of strategy. I do not know much about the game of chess, but what I do know is from James teaching me the game forty three years ago. Thank you, James.

Both my Dad and XMan were millwrights in the paper company and would do welding side jobs in our garage. Everybody and their brother came over to our property for a cold one out of the tap. Everyone would kick back and relax while they all had hitches welded on to their vehicles. Scores and scores of mill workers poured through our garage doors. Many years later I was hired by the same paper mills, and once I arrived, I found many "friends," that had visited our house. The welding operations were so widely known that even vehicles from Grignon's Campers ended up at our house to have work done on them.

In 1972, I became friends with a boy from school by the name of Mark. Mark's dad's name was Keith and he was an electrician in the Prince Edwards division of the Appaloosa Paper Company paper mill. It was an extremely hot summer that year I went over to Mark's house on Lynn Hill road. Mark and I would explore the woods and fields surrounding Fitz's ponds. Mark would then come over to my house so we could find something to do.

One day it was oppressively hot and Mark or I had a book of matches. One of us had the bright idea to drop a lit match into the dry brown grass out in the field just north of Coburn's house. As the brightly colored flames burned a circle outward, it left a small black circle in the center, cool! Once the circle reached a certain size Mark and I would stomp it out so it did not seem like a big deal. Two weeks later I was by myself and I tried the same trick with the matches in the knee deep grass of another field. This time I was by myself behind the go cart track where the hillbillies used to live. Today Bornbach Road passes through that same area.

I stood in the knee high dead brown grass. There had not been a soaking rain for weeks. I pulled the book of forbidden matches from my left side jean pocket. I remember striking the match to the matchbox hearing the ffft sound as I pulled the red tip across the black strike pad. Two weeks earlier, Mark and I mastered burning circles into the grass and then putting them out. But this time I couldn't keep control of the situation. I tried stomping on the flames, but as fast as I stomped, the fire flared up, jumping to a new spot. In panic I began beating the flames with my shirt. "God, please help me!" I shouted. The circles kept growing, three feet, then five feet. I needed help. I hopped on my red bike and pedaled frantically across the old gravel race track to the top of the hill where Pickens lived in the old green house. I was sure Pickens would be home or so I thought as I pounded on their door. It seemed as though an eternity was passing by as I put my ear to the door and listened. I pounded again and again but there was no answer. I rode to the other neighbor's house on the other side of the hill and knocked loudly on their door. Mrs. Peach appeared and I blurted out, "There's a fire across the road out in the field, call the fire department." She said, "You're joking right?" I said, "No, please call the fire department." I then rode my bike down the hill to our house.

My parents were in the house when I told them there was a fire out back. Mom suspected that I was at fault. She was mad as a bobcat as she said, "Steven John, did you start it?" I hung my head in shame and admitted my guilt. At that moment there was no time for talking, only action. Dad had hopped onto his tractor, a Ford 2000 with the double furrow plows. He had already raced toward the field to build fire breaks. He was having considerable success in slowing the fire down before it could get deep into the woods. Dad had been plowing for quite some time before he had any help and as usual his expertise with his tractor paid off. His furrows were slowing the fire so it wouldn't jump the creek and burn everything all the way to Highway 13.

Fire trucks, trucks hauling bulldozers and water tankers began arriving from the Appaloosa Ranger Station and Griffith State Nursery. Sirens were wailing as the big red fire trucks came racing down the road. Up and over the hill they went and out into the field. We ran out back from our house as D.N.R. trucks came onto the scene and began offloading their heavy equipment. To the north was unburnt grass just before the northern woods owned by Lester Smart. The fire to the east began racing towards those woods and the creek.

One of many men unloaded a crawler from the back of a trailer. He quickly crossed hundreds of feet of blackened ground as he headed towards the unburnt grass. He then moved around from one end of the field to the other plowing a separation line all the way into the woods where the fire was still trying to burn. Tongues of yellow, red, and orange flames danced along the end of the field. They were as tall as a man and quickly consumed everything in their path. Fortunately, there was little or no wind. Other heavy equipment could be heard crashing through the woods ahead of the fire. Trees were being knocked over as more furrows were being plowed. Everything was happening so fast! The raging fire devoured the woods, burning up hazel nut brush, jack pines, and various undergrowth. The fire had reached the peak of its fury but now it was beginning to wane. Fire trucks on the back line had moved up and began pumping vast quantities of water into the base of the fire. The firemen were soon gaining ground. Fire trucks on the sides corralled the fire very quickly and the men in the woods completed their fire breaks to put out the flames and disable any hot spots.

Darkness began falling when the fire was completely out. Part of my punishment was experiencing the destructive nature of the fire while the other part of my punishment was to tell the firemen that it was I who had started the fire by playing with matches. My family stayed until the late evening hours watching the men walk around with the water cans on their backs. They kept wetting the ground to kill any remaining live embers and then they left. I walked around in the dark feeling miserable. I was glad the fire was finally out. There is no way that I ever expected to be responsible for the creation of a forest fire. The beautiful circles burnt into the grass turned out to be something ugly once it went out of control.

Something really quite beautiful was found that night in the darkness after the fire. As I walked around the burned area I kicked a log containing phosphorescence. Phosphorescence is a slow emission of light from radiation absorbed in certain materials which lasts but for only a few hours. The light from the log had a white and green glow to it. What I found is really quite rare and finding something so beautiful in a place of destruction was like God saying that no matter how dark a situation might be, He is always there to make something good out of it.

My parents and I quietly walked from the fire scene to the road and then saw that Pickens were home so we stopped by for a while. Mr. Pickens joked around to make me feel better. That is just the way he was, kind, compassionate and understanding.

Looking back I realize there is a lesson here for everyone. Each of us may think that we have our lives all together and under control but we are all guilty of having little faults. Too much laying around and we become lazy, too many fibs and we become liars, excessive speed on the road and we become law breakers, too much alcohol leads to alcoholism, that first cigarette turns into a pack a day and that dope in the needle turns into an addiction. Like matches in dry grass, harmful influences in our lives tend to get away from us.

7

Chapter Seven

The Dry Run

    Lester Smart lived in an old farm house one half mile to the north. It was built in the late 1860's or 1870's and sat on the corner at the intersection of Highway 73 and Strangeline Road. Lester was born June 3, 1924 to Fred and Gertrude Smart and his birthday was on the same day as Klaus Sweeny's. He died of a heart attack while rifle hunting for deer on his beloved oak ridge of the dry run. I believe Lester's grandfather was Gus, who owned land in the creek bottoms of what eventually became to be known as Nepco Lake. Lester had been married more than once and he had several children and step children. When I was growing up Lester happened to be married to a woman named Darcy. She died of cancer in 1987. Lester was with Appaloosa Papers Inc. for forty years and retired in 1986 as a sulphite mill supervisor. Lester was a hardworking, tough talking guy who drank as hard as he worked. He lived hard, and he was a great person to have as a loyal friend. Lester was very opinionated and it did not take very long for him to let you know if he liked you or not. One memory I have of Lester is when he called me Steevie with a cigarette half hanging out of his mouth followed by a half inch of ash ready to fall from the end. Another memory I have is the time when our family and Lester went out to Castle Rock County Park where the flowage is seven miles wide. Lester took us for a ride in his old red and white boat. On that day, he was bleary eyed after having a few too many. His swim suit was sitting low and his beer belly hanging out as he as he ushered us into his boat for a ride across the water. Funny, but when I was growing up people did not think twice about drinking and driving.

Lester had an uncanny resemblance to William Conrad who starred in the television show "Cannon," and later in "Jake and the Fat Man." Lester was rather crude when he spoke. I remember piling wood in XMan's lean to one day while Lester piled wood in the row next to me. He scrutinized my wood piling technique for a few moments. I stopped and stepped back proudly looking at my wood piling progress when all of a sudden I heard him blurt out, "J*sus C*rist, you pile wood like my old lady."

One evening I tried to give myself a haircut while using an electric hair clippers. I used a hand mirror to look in the bathroom mirror to cut my hair, and ended up with a bald spot. Lester happened to be out in the garage so he came to my rescue and gave me a crew cut. Lester liked a short cut for men. Many is the time he would look at the head of hair on a man or boy that he thought was too long and he would call them 'girly boy' or 'honey' to get a rise out of them.

Lester thought that he was tougher than what he really was. I remember one time where several men were cutting firewood out at Henriksen's in the Town of Armenia. Lester was ticked off at XMan so he hauled off and punched him in the mouth giving XMan a fat lip. On another day, Lester was talking tough to my Dad while standing in the opening of XMan's large garage door. I happened to be walking by when I heard my Dad say, "Do you think I can put you down on the ground?" I just kept walking away to look at something but when I turned around Lester was sitting on the ground, sheepishly staring up at me. With Dad twelve years younger and in the prime of his life, he had Lester down on his back in the blink of an eye. Later that night after everyone had enough to drink, Lester's wife Darcy began bragging Lester up. She told my dad that if he was not careful, she would have Lester beat him up. The following words out of Lester's mouth were "Would you shut the h*ll up!"

Lester owned eighty acres of land all the way from the highway and down to Coburn's. He was always out on his John Deere tractor checking on his property. At one time Lester, James Coburn, XMan and Dad had old vehicles which they used for dirt track racing. Dad made a quarter mile oval race track on Lester's land to the north of Coburn's house where they regularly had races. Each driver ran their vehicle as fast as they could through the scrub pines and the field as they rounded the corners. All of us onlookers were standing on the sidelines. Dirt filled the air. We could feel it on our skin, the grit filling our lungs making it difficult to breathe. I could hear Mom scream that the drivers were going too fast as small trees were being rolled over by the tires plowing through the sandy earth. Those really were the good ole days. Men were men and boys were boys. There was no governmental interference or neighbors tattling on each other, just crazy wholesome fun in the neighborhood.

There was an old dried up creek bed on Lester's property which had not seen water in it for forty years. It was the north branch of the Seven Mile and it had been dried up ever since the creation of Nepco Lake. In 1972, XMan bought a small crawler for excavating, when Lester found out he asked my Dad to dig a pond for him down in the hollow deep in the woods. Dad proceeded to dig a small pond which was to become a watering hole for Lester's cows. The length of the pit grew deeper and wider as the crawler moved back and forth pushing the earth into tall banks on each end of the hole. Once the east to west digging was finished it was time to repeat the same process running from north to south. The final result was a pit over fifteen feet deep with a water depth of over four feet.

Major parts of this book are devoted to the natural environment surrounding the land upon which I grew up. I found solace from the nearby fields, woods and streams while I was growing up during periods of loneliness and personal struggles. Hunting of small game, white tail deer, and times of fishing were very therapeutic for me. When I was a boy I used to love hearing stories from the old timers about how the local creeks were all full of swiftly flowing water. Many streams were so cold and deep that they were full of trout. This was before the marshes were ditched to the east in Buena Vista. One elderly man once told me that area was ditched many decades ago to drain the land for agricultural purposes. Before that time, water was so plentiful that Muskies and other large game fish were able to swim three miles upstream in the Five Mile during the spring to spawn. The creek did not start getting shallow until it reached a spot near Pioneer cemetery. Large fish were often found in wagon tracks of settlers after oxen would pull them through the water. Later, a local paper company built Nepco Lake and the watershed covering one hundred and fifty square miles was drained. This took place in 1925 and 1926; when it did the once great streams lost their strength and some branches even dried up. Such was the case of the north branch of my beloved Seven Mile Creek.

Perhaps my interest in how water used to shape the land is why I hold such strong memories of the spring of 1973. It was a very wet spring one week before Easter in April, 1973 as water appeared in places where it had not been seen in nearly fifty years. The marshlands of Buena Vista were so saturated with moisture that the laden land could not shed the water fast enough. The rising water began to find new routes in which to flow and before long the ancient dry creek beds were once again flowing within their banks. That week I wanted to cross the main channel of the Seven Mile in order to explore out behind our house, but the water was too deep. The usually dry basin was covered in water so the only way for me to get across was to climb a hundred feet across the water on the fence of the local game farm. Later that same day I went on a trip to Rapids with Mom, and as we drove, I saw that the dry run was full of water where it crossed Highway 73. As we went north on Highway 13 I saw kids jumping off the edge of the road to swim in the ditch and on my left, the water was flowing through the Camelot Motel. The story was the same another half mile north where the power lines run through another fork of the dry run, how amazing! After our trip, I jumped out of the car and ran as fast as I could to Lester's cow pond to see if there was any water in it. The water came from the east, from Portage County, and moved very slowly where it met every inch of new dry ground. Initially, it moved in a westerly fashion towards the river. It trickled at first but after only a few minutes the water was moving swiftly in the spot where I had been standing. I looked toward the pit and it was completely filled with water.

Being a thirteen year old boy, it seemed like a good idea to find a plank to put in front of the culvert on Strangeline Road. It was not long before the water was flowing several inches deep over the asphalt. None of the drivers traveling down the road seemed to care much because of the momentous occasion of seeing water in the dry run. The next step was for me to run up the road to the store to see if Comet was around. I told him what was happening, so we raced back to the dry run to build an enormous earthen dam. We feverishly shoveled as much dirt as we could down where the water had not yet flowed. Soon the water came up to where we were working. Inch by inch it crept higher until swoosh. Suddenly the water surged forward and all of the dirt was swept away. There was one casualty resulting from our hard labor and that was Comet. When I saw him the next morning in school he was covered in poison ivy from head to toe.

As an adult I have been intrigued by that year of the high water so I have asked many people if they can remember back to that point in time. Unfortunately no one can as it has been forty two years since the great event. I decided to get a map of the area from 1877 and that is when I found the old channels of the Seven Mile. My next step was to visit the local library where I found articles on the subject. One article from May 3, 1973 read "Second wettest April brings another river crest today." It is interesting to note the river crested three times that month. In another article, I read how the water was all of the way up to the home of Mrs. Edith Hodge on Lake Avenue in Grand Rapids; in Saratoga, Tim Jensen, 8, was paddling a canoe in front of the home of his parents on Ranger Road.

Looking back on that summer in the spring of 1973, I chummed around with some classmates from school. There was Roy, who was a foster boy that lived with Eastereggs on Keppler Road, and there was Lyle Broth, who was the son of Richard Broth. Richard worked in the paper mill and then ran his part time plumbing business in the evenings and on weekends. Lyle was allowed to go fishing when he was not being a plumber's helper for his Dad.

School was nearly over and it was our goal to fish all through the summer. Each day we rode our bikes to Getsin's marsh, Ten Mile Creek, Devil's Elbow and Mengels Marsh, Nepco Lake, the Seven Mile Creek and Ten Mile Creek. This area was a fishing paradise for boys in their early teens. Many people from Appaloosa fished Getsin's ponds and a local teacher by the name of Jerry was always walking out from the marsh with largemouth bass or a northern on his stringer. The pan fish were so hungry that for a time the smaller ones would bite on a bare hook. One day Comet and Johann showed up to fish with us, and Roy threw his arm back to cast. The hook caught Comet on the front edge of his eye snapping near his eyeball. Comet screamed bloody murder. That was a very scary moment and it really freaked us out not knowing what had happened. Fortunately, Comet came out of the incident with only a minor scratch.

Faith That Doesn't Burn

It seems that we had a lot of competition on the marsh that year from several very large snapping turtles. Our family was very fond of turtle chowder and fried snapper, so I had a bright idea to create a turtle pole for catching the big creatures. One sunny day I was fishing for pan fish and the stringer was half full. I looked into the water admiring my catch of fish when I noticed a large shadow moving under the water towards the stringer. It was old Mr. Snapper and as I looked down I could see the end of the stringer in his mouth as he tried to swim away with it. There was no real bank in that spot so I was worried about slipping and falling into the water as I lunged toward the stringer. I grabbed hold of it and felt a powerful jerk on the line. The turtle kept tugging at my fish and it became a real struggle for me to retrieve my fish. The whole skirmish took 90 seconds. In the end, I won but the war was not over.

Obviously the turtle was very hungry and very sneaky because every so often I would notice his shadow on the outskirts of the area where I was fishing. I grabbed my wooden turtle pole with the heavy metal wire. Next, I put half of a pan fish on an oversized 2" hook that I had found in my tackle box and attached it to the wire. I cast the bait twenty feet out into the water and then set the turtle pole down. It was then time to get some more real fishing in so I began casting and reeling in more pan fish. Soon the turtle pole lurched towards the water. I scrambled to reach for the pole and once I had it, I tried to pull in the turtle on the wire but it was huge. I sat down on the bank and dug my heels in. With both hands on the pole, I leaned back with all my might, throwing my weight backwards. When the turtle was four feet away I went to give a heave ho to land it on shore. Unfortunately, he gave his neck a quick stretch as he bit onto the wire and cut it in half. Well the turtle disappeared but it was just as well I suppose. I had not thought ahead as to how I would get the snapper to my house while riding my bicycle.

Several days later I went back to the marsh with Roy and Lyle. We cast out little bits of worm on undersized hooks and noticed that small painted turtles were playing out in the water with our bait. As we continued fishing, I realized that we could catch the turtles if we reeled our line in very gently and very slowly. When I headed home that day on my bicycle, there were sixteen turtles in my knapsack, eventually I let the turtles loose in Lester's new pond so the pollywogs and frogs would have company.

8

<u>Chapter Eight</u>

Neighbors

Jason Sculley and his wife Leata were a nice older couple, she being a nurse and Jason working in the beater room at the Prince Edwards paper mill. He grew up off of Hwy. E in Adams County southeast of Adams Friendship and out towards Coloma. His father sold junk and rags for a living during the Great Depression. Mr. Sculley was a pipe smoker, and I remember him chomping on the stem of the pipe trying to get a little extra flavor out of the tobacco. There would be a little drool pooling at the corner of his mouth as he would take his shiny metal cylindrical lighter and squeeze the ends together for ignition and a fresh flame. The Sculley's owned 10.27 acres of land upon which they ran their small hobby farm consisting of a few cows. Out toward the back of the property line was where they dumped their garbage over the years. Interesting articles could be found when scavenging that dump. One such find was a 14 inch figurine of a Japanese man and on the bottom of the statuette was stamped the word Japan. I believe that piece ended up going out with the trash once Mr.

Sculley received the news that his brother had been killed in Pearl Harbor.

Mr. Sculley would rake his lawn every spring but never in the fall. His philosophy was to let leaves and needles lay on the ground over the winter to add nutrients back into the soil. In the spring of 1968, Mr. Sculley had George Sweeny and me help him plant red pines all around his yard. They were growing quite nicely until a new owner took over the property and cut the trees all down. Mr. Sculley was a believer, a born again follower of Jesus Christ, and one of his many accomplishments was to help establish Evergreen Assembly of God on Evergreen Avenue in the town of Saratoga. I will always remember the Sculleys for their easy mannered good nature.

Another family I remember were the Pickens. The Pickens were kindly folks who were always quick with a smile. I remember one year they came to our front door while trick or treating dressed as farmer Brown and his wife. Slim Pickens was the father, and he was employed at the local mill as a truck driver. Heidi worked outside the home at the local canning factory and another food products company. I rarely saw the Pickens and we did not spend much time together; however, their wholesome character had a positive impact on our neighborhood.

Each day after school I would hurriedly hop on my bicycle at our house and ride up and over the hill past Pickens as I sped down the road and over to

Allman's. When I entered their yard, I would coast in with my left foot on the left petal and my right leg over the seat towards the back of the bike. I just could not get there fast enough to surprise Mr. Allman. As I came up to the garage, I would let out my monkey yell, "EE, EE, OOH OOH, AAH, AAH, AAAAH." Mr. Allman would practically drop his cigarette from his left hand and his Point Special beer from his right hand as I burst through the door of his garage. "G*d da*n it, you little pest. You scared the h*ll out of me." That was the affectionate greeting which I received each day when I went to visit them at their house. My relationship with Mr. Allman was much like the cartoon and 1950's television show, "Dennis the Menace." On that show, the neighbor Mr. Wilson, always acted exasperated and put out by Dennis; however, he secretly enjoyed having the young boy around to share his knowledge with. In the Allman household was the father, Gregg Sr., Janet the mother, Anne, who was all grown up and out on her own, Gregg Jr., and Duane. Gregg Jr. was eight years older than me and Duane was two years older.

Gregg Sr. worked for Loverslane Gas Company when I knew him, and he was a jack of all trades. He had an old Whirlitzer juke box in his garage along with a refrigerator to keep Point Special beer cold. A radio was also in the garage and every so often there used to be a jingle which used to go like this, "Point Special beer, Point Special beer, brewed to perfection it taste so good..." As I looked around the garage, I noticed many projects that were being worked on. Other things I remember in the southwest portion of the garage was a little workbench in front of a window. To the left, one could see a blue electronic spark plug cleaning machine. There was also a wood burner toward the back wall in the center of the garage. Mr. Allman spent many hours taking apart appliances and filling empty baby food jars full of the screws, nuts, and bolts. The jars were then hung along the ceiling trusses. On hot summer days, Gregg would have me remain very quiet during the middle of the day. As we listened, I was able to hear what sounded like bees singing. Up in the very highest part of the garage, in the peak of the roof, were nests of wasps rubbing their feet together. They were making music much like crickets do on hot summer nights.

Every year the Allman's had a beautiful garden. It seems to me that Janet did most of the gardening, at least she did a lot of weeding along with the picking of produce. This was a ritual every afternoon for preparation of the evening meal. I never bothered the Allman family while they were eating wanting to leave them alone so as not to disrupt their family time. Instead, I would quietly wait in Duane's bedroom. Once the meal was over, Janet would bring me a couple of large ears of cold corn smothered in butter to eat. There was also a wonderful flower garden in the shape of a triangle between the house and the garage. The flowers were within the perimeter of three sidewalks. I still remember some of the smells of the flowers in the cool of the evening while the dew was falling. At the same time the hummingbirds and Cecropia Moths would fly in. The rapid whirring of their wings would break the stillness of the air around us.

I had a little bit of a relationship with Gregg Jr. Gregg was very smart and he read a lot of books. He was not just book smart but he also was a deep thinker. There would be passages underlined in every book that he read along with personal analytical thoughts. Once the books were completed he passed them on to me and I would read them. My favorite books were "Hiroshima," "A Conneticut Yankee in King Arthur's Court," and "Black Like Me." Gregg was also somewhat of a naturalist and everyday he would go for a long run through the woods on their property.

Duane liked to joke around but he was also serious, especially about his music. He was much disciplined practicing for many hours each day on his steel guitar. I would quietly listen as I sat on his bed. Duane also listened to other country artists for new songs to play. Some of my favorite songs were, "You've Got to Kiss an Angel Good Morning "by Charlie Pride and, "There Ain't No Corn on Rocky Top." I think that song was done by Dolly Parton and later; the Nitty Gritty Dirt Band. Two other songs that come to mind were "Cocaine Blues" and "Folsum Prison" by Johnny Cash.

Some of my other recollections of Duane were of the time when he shot a deer with his bow out in the dead oak wilt west of their field, and when he purchased   the red Cushman scooter that my Dad once owned and Duane's Suzuki 125 off -road on - road motorcycle. Duane also had a job just down the road at the local game farm along with his friend Gary. For entertainment, Gary used to blow up Mr. Smedstead's bird houses with fire crackers and M80's. One of the final memories I have is of Duane's black Mach I Mustang. Duane was a good guy and the All-mans were great people.

My dad woke up the first night that we moved onto Strangeline Road. The windows were open, and he was awakened to the sound of a woman scream-ing in the distance, or so he thought. He walked around the house and looked out into the woods but could not see anything, so he went back to bed and fell back asleep. It was not very long before the same thing happened again, the hysterical screaming from deep in the woods. This went on all throughout the night. The next day Dad did some investigating and found out that a neighbor down the road had pea-cocks at his game farm. That was what had created the wailing sounds all night long. The game farm was on land formerly owned by Gust Brown which was later purchased by Regis Smedstead. In the previous chapter, I wrote about the north branch of the Seven Mile to the north of our house but the game farm property to the south held a beautiful pond located on the south branch of the Seven Mile.

The Smedstead's owned a very nice home with

a cabin type exterior on a rise overlooking the water. West of the house was a cottage down by the water. In the cottage were all kinds of stuffed fish, birds and animals. The Smedstead property amounted to one hundred and seven acres. There were forty acres west of Strangeline road, and on the east side were sixty seven acres, of which approximately fifty acres made up the game farm. I remember seeing llamas, white tailed deer, pheasants, ducks, geese, swans, raccoons, and fox. There may have even been black bear, along with other types of animals. Regis was an entrepreneur and businessman who knew how to manage many types of business ventures, so it is no surprise that he owned the Regis Pleasing Supermarket store in Appaloosa. Each day he brought home expired produce in the afternoon to feed his animals.

The history of the Smedstead property is rather interesting. In a 1940s edition of "The Wisconsin Rapids Daily Tribune" is an article titled, "Waters of Seven Mile Creek Form Town of Saratoga Lake" and reads as follows:

> "Only about a month ago Seven- Mile creek meandered its way through Sections 18 and 19 of the town of Saratoga, its waters running in a southwesterly direction and dumping into the Wisconsin River.
>
> Today a lake has been created along part of the streams course, and although small, promises to become one of the most beautiful small bodies

of water in central, Wisconsin.

Creation of the lake - it has not yet been given a name - was undertaken over a month ago by W. A. Radke and J.L. Swinghammer, Nekoosa sportsmen. They purchased 97 acres of property, including the lake bed and land adjoining which had been owned by Gust Brown.

In this section of land the two men saw the possibilities of damming the creek's flow, flooding an area of about 20 acres in the bed which the land topography indicates the stream had originally flowed. This would provide the advantages of natural shorelines.

On the east side of a town road... two men constructed a concrete dam with a 9 – foot spillway which has a height of 14 feet...

Since the stream is spring – fed, the lake's waters are clear and cold. As a recreational project, Mr. Radke and Mr. Swinghammer contemplate the planting of trout and wild rice for wild fowl and fish food..."

I remember during the drought of 1987 – 1989 when most of his pond dried up. Regis could not believe it was possible because "those springs flowed all the way from Canada." It was impossible for the lake to dry up! I do not know what year Regis bought the property from Gust Brown, but he sure fell into a wonderful opportunity which afforded him many years of pleasure. Regis was originally from Green Bay where he was born on Sept. 6, 1911 to Albert and Ester. In doing a search of the owner's real surname I found possible relatives in Door County. At any rate, Regis must have been exposed to a good dose of nature as a child because as a young man, wildlife became his passion. Regis was a real character and the final authority in all matters. Whenever he spoke it was to make a point and when he finished a sentence he would look at you and say, "Right?"

Over the years I would often visit with some of my former neighbors, and I would bring some of my children along to meet those wonderful people from the old neighborhood. On one particular day in 1996, I took my twelve year old son Caleb to Smedstead's house and Regis invited us in. I had not seen him for twenty years so of course he was much older, but he was still saying "Right, right?" We sat at his kitchen table and then the elderly gentleman began bragging about what great shape he was in and he began flexing his muscles. Regis then told Caleb and me to feel how hard his muscles were. We were looking at one another in silence when suddenly Regis challenged Caleb to an arm wrestling match. I really felt uncomfortable with Caleb arm wrestling an eighty five year old man, but Regis kept insisting. It became obvious that we would not be allowed to leave unless the match took place. Caleb and Regis did indeed have the match, a twelve year old boy and an eighty five year old man; the match ended in a draw.

My fondest memory of the Seven Mile takes place one summer day in 1972. Regis allowed fishing in his pond by neighbor boys but only if they weeded the quack grass first from his nursery. Kneeling amongst the evergreens and shrubs and pulling quack grass while the hot sun beat down was no easy task. Regis of course wanted every white quack root to be picked up as he stood overhead supervising the job. He talked about the quality of work that he expected. Standing overhead, he gave his life philosophies and expected me to be his yes man. At times I wondered if it was worth listening to Regis for so long just to fish for a couple of hours, but on one particular day, it all became worthwhile. On that day the weeding was done so I ran down the sidewalk, past the kitchen window, through the patio, and around the large fish tank, full of native bass and pan fish. Down below the hill was an old tin boat and in the boat lay my fishing pole along with the tackle box and container of worms. Was I ever ready to fish! The day before, another boy by the name of Mark had a fish on his line that was longer than our arms. It fell off the line as we were getting the net to bring it into the boat.

Nature played out all around me on Regis's pond. One day I went fishing and cast out an orange French spinner out over the water next to a willow tree. The lure began dropping, and as it did so, an oriole swooped down and swallowed it. Many times, I could see fish swimming on the bottom of the lake as I looked over the edge of the boat. Just above the golden sand were bluegills, pumpkin seeds, crappies, perch and occasionally a large mouth bass. The big bass would cruise like torpedoes, lurking between the shallows and the great deep. The pond was long and fairly wide so on a windy day the boat would drift along allowing us to troll the waters. It was easy to catch largemouth bass on daredevils, French spinners, rapalas, lead jigs, minnows and worms. It seemed like the fish bit on almost anything. It really did not take much to provoke the large fish into biting as they were very aggressive.

On this day of fishing, I cast out with a large yellow orange lead jig. Suddenly, I had a big fish on. It felt like a log at first and then the line broke. What a bummer! I was excited though, and my heart raced as I tied another leader and jig onto the line. I cast out once again and the jig hit the water with a loud Ker plunk. I began reeling in the line, and as I did so, another fish hit; bang! It pulled back and forth, tugging and splashing as I wrestled the monster into the boat. What a beauty it was, a young boy's trophy. I took my belt off and slipped it through the massive gills so I could ride home with it on my bike. The fish was nineteen inches long and weighed nearly six pounds. Dad was so proud of me that he gave me his tackle box with all of his baits in it. Smedstead's pond is no more. One year the stone bridge was removed from Strangeline Road. A bridge nearly as old as, and similarly built like the historical bridge at Historic Point Basse on Wakely Road in Saratoga. Years later, the town removed the spillway holding back the water. Not only was Smedstead's pond finally eliminated but the entire Seven Mile Creek upstream has also been greatly diminished. In Portage County, the Seven Mile Creek and Ten Mile Creek ran together as a drainage ditch until a field was created and the creek bed filled in. This occurred where the Seven Mile forks off from the beginning of the Ten Mile Creek, thus killing the once great trout stream. Soon no one will remember the importance of those once great waterways and the memories they hold for those of us who lived there.

9

Chapter Nine

A Fork in the Road

The following is a series of events which took place toward the end of my junior high years. It is at this point where I go from childhood into adolescence before high school begins. The wrong choices made in choosing friends and improper decision making were about to take me down a road that had serious consequences.

I believe XMan's block garage was built right next door to our home property in August of 1970. Sometime time later he began putting cement ring casings deep into the ground on our property for a well in back of Dad's garage. One fall day we were digging and hauling up the buckets of sand in order to make the well deeper. Our attention turned to the sound of geese loudly honking in the distance as they began their approach to Smedstead's pond. Soon the large birds would begin their descent over our property in order to land. XMan said, "Steve, go get the long Tom from the garage." Now the long Tom was a twelve gauge shotgun with a very long barrel, and it was ideal for shooting geese. I ran toward the garage to get the gun but my sister Sherry decided to take that honor from me. Why she went to get the gun I will never know. Sherry was only ten years old at the time and had no business handling a gun that was bigger than she was. With a generous head start she tried to out run me as she entered the garage and reached out to grab the gun.

Sherry fought for control of the gun and would not let me have it, but I was told to bring the gun and I was willing to do anything for XMan's acceptance. I squeezed my sister's neck from behind like Dad used to do to me when he was annoyed. Sherry let go of the gun and ran out of the garage and into the back yard where everyone was waiting. She stood there crying as I brought the gun from the garage and handed it to XMan. I was then told to go into the house and get something from the basement. I entered the house and descended the basement steps. I turned left and walked toward the freezer and that is when Dad appeared from behind me; was he ever furious.

I cannot remember what Dad said to me about making Sherry cry. All I can remember is fear; fear of the frustration in his eyes and fear of the anger on his face as he yelled at me. I also cannot remember what Dad did to me. I was not being punched or slapped or spanked or kicked. It was more like being laid out on my back on the cement floor as he grabbed me and shook me up and down. I guess I was being shaken violently. I became scared, upset, and then mad as I ran up the stairs and out into our garage. My feelings were really hurt so I hopped on my bike and headed for Appaloosa. I wanted to get as far from that house as possible. I was so mad and frustrated at not having any adults in my life, adults who were pleased with me. I had no relationship whatsoever with the people living in our house. There was a pile of rocks left over from replacing our septic drain field and half of that pile was gone. I had been using those rocks up each day after school by throwing them at jack pines. That is how I was able to deal with my frustrations after school or when I was angry at my parents. But now so many thoughts were racing through my mind and I needed to spend some time alone.

I furiously rode my bicycle down Strangeline Road towards Highway 73 and headed west for Appaloosa. I had been standing on my bicycle pedals and I raised up each time that I pedaled in order to go faster. Without warning the bicycle chain slipped off as I approached Wagon Wheel Drive. I was going at least fifteen miles per hour as I lost control of my bike and flew shoulder first onto the blacktop and loose gravel. My knees and elbows dug into the hard surface as the blacktop tore my skin and ripped into my flesh. I stood there crying along the side of the road when suddenly a car appeared alongside me; it was Duane Allman. He asked me if I was ok and offered me a ride home. I am fifty six years old and I am tearing up as I write this because of the compassion Duane showed me on that day. I also tear up when I think about how much God loves me. God sent Duane to help me in my time of need. It was not a coincidence that Duane showed up at the exact moment when I needed help; God sent him! When people of faith get to a certain age they can see how the hand of God has intervened in their life over the years. God really does exist. He loves us and He takes care of us. I do not know how people make it through this life without Him.

Duane took me home after the bicycle mishap and by that time Dad had mellowed out a bit. I went into the house and headed for my bedroom. I sat on my bed as Dad appeared in the doorway. He tried to have "a talk," you know, where I am talked at but not talked with, where he talks and I listen, the speech where I should not have done this or I should not have done that... and how he was only trying to get my attention. In my childhood years growing up, Dad never once sat on the edge of my bed to have a conversation with me. We never talked at the kitchen table or in the living room or while going places. I do not ever remember having a father and son conversation except for the one time that we were digging worms and found the salamander. I do not blame Dad for our lack of a relationship because Dad never experienced any quality time with his Dad. As for Dad's anger in the basement, well, let's just say that it was misdirected at me. His frustrations were mounting daily due to the fact that he kept getting the short end of the stick.

I believe that day of the long Tom was a turning point for my mother as she was deciding in her heart how to protect us kids. She had drifted away from her husband emotionally, A husband she no longer understood or cared to know, and yet those virtues were exactly what Dad needed in his life. It was now just a matter of time before Mom's plans of escape would become a reality. There are people who blamed Mom for mistakes that she had made. There were people who judged me for the mistakes which I had made, and there are people who judged Dad for the way that he was. I have learned that some of our mistakes are generational, a generational curse if you will, and sometimes that curse can be broken only by the power of God through Jesus. I completely understand where my Dad was at mentally and emotionally all of those years before he found Jesus; I know the how and whys of his behavior. Years ago I found Dad's testimony of the struggles he faced before finding Jesus and here are some excerpts from some of his former notes:

> " Until I was forty two years old I never
> had peace of mind and I cannot ever
> remember being happy. I was born on a
> farm and as far back as I can remember I
> was full of anger and resentment. I don't
> know why I was angry but my Dad was a
> drunk and I was the fourth child and the
> experts say that the fourth child doesn't
> get any attention. My Dad was hardly
> ever around and when he was he was

*drunk. He always got ugly when he was
drunk. He always picked on my mom and
maybe that is where the anger started, I
don't know."*

Roger and Deb Gerzmehle had lived in Sweeny's house for about a year before they moved into the house at the corner of Point Basse and Elm Street where Roger grew up in Appaloosa. The Gerzmehles had a personal relationship with Jesus, something that I knew nothing about. What is a relationship with Jesus anyway? The Gerzmehles belonged to "Youth for Christ" so they invited me to come over to their house for activities with other youth in the community. I would ride my bike the four miles to their house. From there, we would visit homes of the elderly and do fall yard work for them. Everyone would meet back at Gerzmehles for hot chocolate once we were done with our random acts of kindness and soon a bible study would follow. Everyone had a Bible but me; strange but in our Catholic home I never saw a Bible anywhere. I really wanted to know God the way other kids in that bible study knew Him, but the things they talked about just went right over my head. Had I ever prayed a sinner's prayer and invited Jesus into my heart? Did I know him? I think not.

As a Catholic I prayed to Mary, saints, and angels but not Jesus, although I do remember vague prayers with the word "Lord" used in them. In the Catholic Church I never really heard anyone pray to Jesus much less pursue a personal relationship with

Him. His name was used in the Apostle's Creed which is a really good prayer and it's mentioned briefly in a couple parts of the mass. I heard repetitious prayers read from a missalette or recitations with the rosary, but I never heard anyone talk to Jesus like you would a friend. Parishioners in the church heard the name of Jesus just like you hear about the President, governor or mayor but how many church goers are friends with those kinds of officials? How many people really know the saving power of Jesus blood and have a friendly daily relationship with Him? How many people really know Him? Mary, the mother of Jesus, had a really good piece of advice that we should heed; she said, "Whatever He says to you, do it" (John 2:5). So when Jesus says that we must be born again in John 3:7 then we must obey him and do so. As believers we also need to read the Bible every day in order for us to obey the commands and directives that Jesus has for each one of us. How else can we know what His expectations and his will are?

I suppose I was a mommy's boy growing up because Dad and I had a nonexistent relationship. I have several memories of her being distraught such as the time when President JFK died; he was Catholic you know. Many Catholics were devastated, not just because he was our President and died but also because he was a President of the Catholic faith. Another memory I have is of Mom one summer afternoon when she was sitting on the front steps of our house and she was crying. She had just received a phone call that her grandmother had passed away. On another day I royally upset Mom by smarting off. She grabbed a yardstick to give me a spanking so I tore out of the garage and ran into the front yard to get away from her. Mom could not catch me so she yelled out, "You are going to get it when your father comes home." When Dad came home he told her to spank me herself, he was tired of always having to be the "bad guy."

There were often Snapping Turtles kept as prisoners in 55 gallon steel barrels in the front yard. Lurking in the water at the bottom, they were awaiting the executioner who would cut their heads off with an ax so we could turn them into fried turtle or turtle chowder. You had to wait at least 24 hours to clean the turtle because the heart was still beating and the legs would occasionally move when you touched them. Once the turtle was opened up we would separate the many types of meat from the innards. Later us kids would collect the eggs and bury them in the sand and wait for them to hatch.

We used to go to grandma Bornbach's when she butchered chickens. As kids it was our job to pick off the pin feathers and pull the yellow skin out of the gizzards. When grandma butchered pigs it was my job to come along with a bowl and catch blood flowing from the neck to make blood sausage.

I remember one time Dad went up to Ashland for the smelt run and he came back with a 55 gallon barrel full of smelt. We would cut off their heads with a scissors and make a slit up their belly then us kids would clean them up inside and out with tooth brushes.

Lester Smart had a step daughter by the name of Rhonda. One of Rhonda's hobbies was to melt different colored crayons over glass bottles for decorations; she also played with the Ouija board. After many years of drugs and darkness I say that many "harmless" games are gateways into the occult. What do you think makes those pieces move on the board?

One night we heard sirens half a mile away so we ran down our driveway to the edge of the road and looked north towards Highway 73. The sky was ablaze from a garage on fire. The next day we found out that it was at Chickadees, their daughters Juanita and Drusilla were my classmates at school.

Dad owned several tractors over the years. There was the orange Allis Chalmers, a gray Ford Ferguson 30, a blue Ford 2000, and then an orange propane powered Minneapolis Moline. Dad's current tractor is his Ford 4000 which he once used to drag snowmobile trails and build a bridge. Now he uses it to plow snow from his driveway. He also removes snow for his neighbors in the winter and they love him for it.

The parents used to go out every Friday evening for fish fry's but on one particular night they stayed out quite late. My siblings and I ended up staying over at Sweeny's house where we were watching the movie Godzilla. Godzilla was just coming up out of the water by a little coastal village. The people were scurrying to get away but one woman did not make it. Godzilla reached down picked her up and then ate her. This was happening at the same time that Klaus Sweeny burst through their kitchen. Godzilla was spitting the woman's red dress out of his mouth as Klaus began talking loudly in a rather excited manner. Klaus said that a group of kids were at our house trying to steal gas from the gas pump. He ran out to his brown Jeep International Scout and we followed in hot pursuit of the gas thieving bandits. The Jeep tore up the asphalt with the speedometer reading eighty as we headed south on Strangeline Road. We hit the dirt fire lanes at the top of Seven Mile Creek while in hot pursuit but ate dust as the thieves eventually outran us. A couple of nights later my Dad was standing in the dark doorway of his garage when suddenly the same group of teenagers pulled up to the pump again. Those kids were so doped up that when my Dad stepped out from the shadows to ask them what they were doing, they replied," We are here to get some gas." Dad then told them to go home and from that day on he kept the gas pump locked.

Death is a fact of life and it seemed as though there was plenty of death to go around while I was growing up. Great grandpa Linzmeier lived north

of Blenker, Wisconsin near the intersection of May-
flower and Yellowstone roads. He died in 1969 but I
still remember the funeral and the casket being lowered into the ground at the cemetery in back of St.
Killian's church. Not long afterwards great grandma
Bornbach broke her hip and within a year she died.
I remember staring into her casket at Rembs funeral home and waiting for her to open her eyes and
reach out to grab me. Death was scary. Another great
grandma soon died and it was the same story in Daul
Town: dying, funerals and then coffins being lowered
into the ground. Where did those people go when
their spirit left the body? Those who know Jesus have
an assurance from the bible which says this, "To be
absent from the body is to be present with the Lord"
(2 Corinthians 5:8). The Bible does not make a case
for believers to be sent to a waiting place until they
become good enough to enter heaven.

It was not just the elderly who died but also
the young. I remember when a boy named Jerold
died when I was in sixth grade. I did not know the
boy but I heard the tragic story of how he died. The
details are blurry, was he drinking, was he racing, was
his liver really hanging in a tree? I do remember going
to the crash site and seeing how the airborne car
snapped the red pines off ten to twelve feet up from
the ground. I have the article from the crash on Sep-
tember 13, 1971. The officers on the scene had never
seen such a mangled pile of metal as Jerold's vehicle.
Jerold was only 17 and his passenger Terrance was
24.

A few years later I went bow hunting with the Simpson boys out in Juneau County and the hunting party was made up of several young men. In a short period of time many people in that age group suddenly died. One guy who was a friend of Bob Crust died of leukemia. Another fellow, Will Plankmore, died in an automobile crash on the curve of Highway 73 by Wyandotte Chemical Plant. A third fellow by the name of John died at the paper mill in the sewer along with two other men from the paper mill; they were overcome by hydrogen sulfide gas. My dad would have been the next victim. As a Millwright in charge of machine repairs he thought that he might be able to rush in to save the others. He too would have been overcome by the poisonous gas and there would have been yet another funeral for me to go to. I am glad Dad lived so we could know one another as adults. He has taught me so many valuable lessons over the last thirty seven years. It would make me happy if I could ever become even half the Godly man that Dad is.

One night I remember going to bed when I was twelve years old. I had been trying to go to sleep after I said my guardian angel prayer. For some reason my mind would not relax and my heart raced as I began wondering what would happen to me if I died. It was very upsetting for me not to know, so I left my bed and walked out to the living room. I saw Mom sitting on the couch watching television, so I asked her what happens to people after they die; she did not know.

Death can be cruel but people can be just as mean and cruel. One of our classmates by the name of Crist Flue was having a birthday; he was turning thirteen. Crist was really excited about his special day and he went around sharing all day long that it was his birthday. The school bell rang at the end of the day and Crist was standing by the front steps of the school with students who were waiting for their bus to arrive. Crist continued to tell other students that it was his birthday until Chuck showed up at the bottom of the steps. He said, "Crist I have a present for you." Then he proceeded to give Crist a birthday present with his fists. I do not know exactly what Chuck did to poor Crist but he beat him so bad that Crist was taken away by an ambulance.

Many events took place in my life from 1973 – 1975. In seventh grade I went out for wrestling and I joined the Boy Scouts. In those two events I made friends with Johann Keppler and Bart Simpson. As for wrestling, let's just say that I stank. I never won a match and I resembled a fish flopping out there on the mat. Our coaches Ron Ystad and Gordy Freeman were very good coaches, but I just could not see without my glasses. I am such a slow learner when it comes to grasping wrestling moves. Johann Keppler was a goody two shoes and a mommy's boy; Bart Simpson was trouble and nobody's boy. Both guys had a good sense of humor and were interesting to be around. Johann was a very good wrestler. He was very strong and much disciplined, he worked out on rings that hung down from the ceiling in his basement. I hung around with Johann for about a year and the last time I saw him was the night that I was spanked with a 2x4 from my Dad's hand.

One Friday night I went to a football game in Appaloosa and there I met Comet Kohotek and Bart Simpson. We were bored and looking for some excitement so we took the trail in the dark from Pischke Elementary School up to the high school track. On the way, Bart found a girls coat laying on the ground, so he tried it on to see if it fit. Comet and I tried to pull the coat off of Bart but it was on so tight that it ripped. Once the coat came off it dropped to the ground so we left it and went back to watch the game. Later we encountered two police officers who were walking towards the athletic field. They rounded us up and drove us to headquarters for interrogation. Bart said, "Don't tell them anything, they've got nothing on us." We were all put into separate rooms and an officer by the name of Ken Ruder began questioning me. I spilled the beans; I just could not bring myself to lie. I really liked officer Ruder and over the years I found him to be a friendly man and full of integrity. He has my deepest admiration. The girl who owned the coat was Barbi Benton and her father worked with my dad in the paper mill. Comet, Bart, and I each had to pay five dollars to replace the coat.

Comet Kohotek lived at the intersection of Highway73 and Strangeline Road where his family ran a little country grocery store. One night Johann Keppler, Comet, and I were together were looking for some excitement, so we grabbed a five gallon bucket full of tomatoes to throw at cars. I do not know where the tomatoes came from but they were readily available to use as ammunition. I said earlier that Johann wasn't much for getting into trouble but Comet was no chicken and usually took a dare. I really do not know who threw the first tomato, but I was not about to be outdone. I threw as many tomatoes as I could at cars moving down the highway. Motorists were locking up their brakes and honking as they passed by but one vehicle stopped and a bunch of guys piled out and tore after us. We split up and ran in different directions. I headed south through the red pines and into thick hazelnut brush. I saw a flashlight and I heard the group that was searching for me. They were standing just ten feet away, so I thought the loud beating of my heart would give away my hiding place. They lingered just a minute longer and then took off. I headed back to the store and found Johann. Then we headed back toward my house. When we were about a hundred yards from the house, I turned towards Johann and said, "I sure am glad those guys did not catch me." No sooner were the words out of my mouth when Dad met me in the driveway with a 2x4 in his hand. Mom then appeared and said, "Steven John, were you throwing tomatoes at cars?" My silence was an admission of guilt. Mom told Johann to go home and he took off on his moped like a scared rabbit running from a rabid wolf. XMan's garage was full of company as Dad marched me in through the door and turned out the lights. Each time the force of the board hit my behind I yelped and with each whack my voice went up an octave higher. Well I got my beating, but it did no good. I never would have been running the streets if I had a dad that I could spend time with, so nothing changed.

There is a lesson to be learned here for adults and that is, it is impossible to beat sense into a kid. I was beat with a wooden playpen slat when I needed glasses, I was beat until one of my butt cheeks was black and blue when I was little and did not come in to get cleaned up for bed time. I was roughed up on the basement floor because of my sister and the shotgun and I was beat with a 2x4 for throwing tomatoes at cars. A person needs a change of heart for real authentic change to take place in one's life; that only happens with time and love from others, and last but not least, help from God.

A friend and I climbed onto XMan's garage roof. We wanted to lay on our backs up there and watch the stars. Was that such a crime? Here I am, staying home and having good clean innocent fun. Dad saw me on the roof and said, "You're going to get it when you come into the house." For crying out loud, there is just no winning with that guy so I waited outside for a very long time. Later, I headed into the house and quietly made my way through the kitchen then into the bathroom and from there I cut across the hall and went into my bedroom without Dad seeing me.

I figured that I would not get a beating if everyone thought I was sleeping. I laid in bed waiting to see what would happen. All of a sudden I heard my dad say, "When is he coming in here?" Then mom said, "He went to bed a long time ago," and that was the end of it. From that time on I avoided any kind of contact with my Dad for the next four years. When I was seventeen I moved away and I did not intend to see him ever again, but God had different plans for both of us.

I was fifteen years old when I started my first real summer job. It was trimming Christmas trees with a long knife. Each day I would wake up early in the morning and walk half a mile to the highway. Once there, I would wait for my ride from the other boys who lived in Appaloosa. They felt it was not worth their time to pick me up or to drop me off at my house, even though I paid a fee of 50 cents each day for the trip. The driver of the blue Camaro was Tim Brost. The other passengers were Jay Faulkner, Ross Miltimore and Dave Gildenzoph. Since I was the youngest, my assigned spot was to sit on the hump over the pumpkin in the back seat. Our destination each day was Peals Tree farm located 3.5 miles north of Plainfield. It was a 22 mile drive one way.

Each morning we would pull in to the company site. From there we would ride in the work bus to various pine tree plantations throughout Waushara County. Once we reached our destination we would put on our red shin guards. With our long knives, we made downward sweeping motions to cut the tree laterals and side branches into a uniform triangle shape to make Christmas trees. It was so hot and sweaty in those plantations as we battled bugs and bees. Whenever the temperature hit ninety degrees we were sent home.

Our foreman was a rather arrogant individual who liked to talk down to people. He liked to pick fights with high school and college aged tree trimmers. I have heard from past workers on other crews that he would pick fights to show off and impress the girls. Now the foreman's name was Moe Peeler and he had been in the army. Moe thought he knew everything there was to know about taking a man down and controlling him into submission. On one particular day Moe was bragging as he looked at Dave Gildenzoph. He said, "I bet I can take you down to the ground and you can't stop me." Dave looked at Moe and said, "Go ahead and try." In the blink of an eye Moe was on the ground. He did not know what hit him. As it turns out, Dave had gone to state as a middle weight wrestler for the Papermakers.

Bart Simpson was perhaps the longest lasting friend that I had during my teen age years. He smoke, drank, and did drugs but he was such a friendly easy going person. I really liked the guy. There was also Homer Simpson his Dad, Marge Simpson his mom, an older brother named Floyd who always pounded on Bart, and his younger sister was Maggie. One day Bart and Floyd had the bright idea to have an all-out fight with crab apples. Floyd was no match for my rock throwing arm so he disappeared into the house but then reappeared a few moments later. Floyd was holding a wrist rocket in his hand as he ran up to the white oak in the back yard. Bending down he deftly loaded the wrist rocket with a large acorn. Floyd suddenly rose up, and turned towards me as he pulled back the rubber sling and took aim. I saw the look of concentration and his wicked grin, so I began running away. Instantly I felt large acorns pelting my back and soon had a trophy welt before I left for home.

Homer was a person who really had an impact on my life and I really appreciated him. Homer was a real bright spot even though the rest of my life was mud. He did not tear me down, he built me up. He ministered to my self-esteem. I looked forward to his greeting every time I went to his house. He would look up from his newspaper as soon as he heard my voice when I entered their living room and proclaimed, "Hello professor." You see, Homer saw something in me that no one else did, potential! Yes that is true, potential. No I am not all that bright, but Homer saw my love for science, geography, history and trivial facts. He wanted to see me cultivate those wholesome quality subjects that I was gifted in. He did not want me to throw my life away with drugs. Over the next few years I made many wrong choices. I feel like I let Homer down because I succumbed to the lure of drugs. Decades later I went to visit Homer each time that I noticed him sitting in his back yard. His greeting was always the same, "Hello professor." Homer died in the summer of 2015, and I miss him.

10

Chapter Ten

Darkness is Falling

Have you ever made promises to God that were not kept? You know what I mean. God, if you do me this one small favor then I will... I went to mass every Sunday and many times I sat in the pew promising God that I would never lie, smoke, drink, steal, swear or do drugs. Guess what, I lied.

My first day as a freshman in high school started out as follows: 7:30 A.M. I walked downstairs to the boy's bathroom from the commons area. Dick Van Patten was waiting to greet me as I passed through the bathroom doors. As soon as I made eye contact, Dick responded by hacking up a huge wad of phlegm and spit it onto my shirt collar. What a pig! I had never seen that guy before and that is the kind of greeting I received on my first day of high school. Two other guys walked into the bathroom as I was scrubbing sputum off from my shirt. They were a couple more upper classmen by the name of Lee Van Cleef and Gary Cooper. They looked at me and at the same time each one took a six shot revolver from their lunch boxes. Making sure I saw them. The guns were supposedly for a project in metals class. From there, I went to my first hour class, I went to Applied 1 Math, and met the teacher. His name was Richard Dreyfus. Mr. Dreyfus had no use for me once he found out that I was not going out for any sports. Oh well, who needs an education anyway, obviously football is more important. From that day on for the rest of the school year, I was not worth Richard's time. I did make friends with some teachers as the years went on. Jim Matthias, Thomas Schider, and Ruth Macomber were priceless individuals who showed genuine interest in me as a person.

I had been hanging around with the Simpson boys for a whole year while they were getting high and they seemed ok to me. The Simpsons and I listened to many different musical artists and some of the music was dark and sadistic. Alice Coopers 'Killer' album with the rattle snake on the cover and the song "Dead Babies" is really not exactly wholesome entertainment material. Black Sabbath also had music that could really drag your soul into the pit of Hell. Lead singer Ozzy Osbourn always seemed to relish his title, "The Prince of Darkness," and some of his lyrics reinforce that image. I remember the song "Sabbath Bloody Sabbath" and its lyrics went as follows,"

Nobody will ever let you know, when you ask the reason why. They just tell that you're on your own, fill your head all full of lies... No more tomorrow, life is killing you; Dreams turn to nightmares; Heaven turns to Hell, burned out confusion, nothing more to tell."

A lot of things look ok before they take control and choke the life out of you. The Simpsons and I listened to Black Sabbath music and Alice Cooper's "Killer" album with "Dead babies," along with songs from other artists. People do not realize it but our mind is like a computer but we must choose: garbage in means garbage out. What we choose to see and hear does impact our thoughts and actions. People can argue the point all they want but have you ever awakened at night to use the bathroom and find yourself thinking of a song that you heard the day before or perhaps remember a movie that you saw right before bedtime? When you do drugs and allow an evil mindset from bad lyrics into your mind, it affects you, it destroys your values, and it takes away hope and alienates you from God.

I listened to songs of hopelessness and despair; add to that no relationship with my parents, and the crap I put up with at school and life in general became pretty depressing. One day I stepped off of the school bus and noticed Barry Williams leaning out of the school bus window. He produced a large fat rubber band loaded with a big paper clip. There was no time for me to react as the projectile was launched towards me. Can you imagine the pain I felt in my face upon impact by the paper clip?

Speaking of pain, how about phy-ed class? Robert Conrad was our gym instructor in my freshman year of high school. He allowed certain liberties for students with athletic abilities. Those special students were allowed to basically bully, pick on, and abuse whoever was of a lower standing in the pecking order of life. Unfortunately, Ken Curtiss, Don Knott's, and I were considered the lowest life forms in that class. This was never more evident than in the process of the alphabet game. As Mr. Conrad looked the other way, "Conrad's athletes" would corner their next unsuspecting victim and drop him to the ground. The perpetrators would pull the boy's shirt up over his chest and the torture would then begin. With multiple hands the masters of pain would slap the victims belly shouting the letter "A," then "B," all the way through the 26 letters of the alphabet. If the person being slapped yelled out, the process would begin all over again beginning at the letter "A." It is for reasons such as this that many adults do not participate in class reunions. For them, memories of school are only filled with memories of pain. I remember how the other boys treated Don Knotts shouting "Hey Kotex" each time Don entered a room. I do not know how Don rose above that stigma. Fortunately, I have been able to rise above the past and I wish the very best for each of my former classmates.

Well, what about religion you might ask, surely religion makes life better. That is laughable. Here is what religion did for me: I was a junior in high school and one night we were at CCD religion classes (catechism instruction) at Irwin's home on Lynn Hill Road in Appaloosa. My hair was getting longer and I twirled my fingers in it a couple of times which really irritated Mick Fresh. He and my male classmates decided they were going to give me a beating after class. I did not know this was going to happen until class was over. As I began to I walk out the door, something threatening was said to me. My instinct told me that it was time to run for my life. Babe Ruth was the ring leader along with Mick Fresh, Crosby, Stills, Nash, and Young... their goal was to hunt me down in the dark. Babe Ruth was leading the pack and they ran like hounds with the smell of blood in their senses after a fox. I ran along the road in the darkness and then jumped down into the ditch hoping to hide in the long grass. The pack lost my trail and began to double back, so I jumped up and began running again until I reached the steps of a farm house. I began pounding on the door but no one was home. The group approached me with Babe taking the lead. He came in close and slugged me in the gut to make made sure I knew who the boss was, and then they left.

I went to a thirty-five year class reunion last summer. While I was there, Babe made it a point to brag to me about what he had done to me that night so very long ago. My response was to send him a nice card the next day telling him that I forgave him. Looking back in retrospect, I too was no angel. Just a few days before that CCD meeting, I had punched Wally Cleaver in the mouth. I was sick of him swearing at me every day that year in school. He would call me F*cker; or F*cking a *s hole. There came a point where I could no longer take any more crap from

Wally so I slugged him in the mouth. Wally missed the next several days of school. I suspect Wally was Babe's friend and my beating after CCD may have been payback time for what I had done. Oh well, what goes around comes around.

I had been hanging around with the Simpsons for a whole year before I decided that I would get high with them. Floyd Simpson was a couple of years older than I was and his older brother Bart was three years older. One day Floyd's buddy Quirt Evans stopped by to pick up Floyd, and they were going to take a ride. (Back in the 70's, taking a ride meant leaving the house to get high.) Quirt invited Bart and me to also ride along. We took a trip past Twin Lakes in Adams County and ended up by some kind of wooden platform or outlook near Chicago Avenue. We parked the car and climbed up onto the platform. Quirt then rolled a joint and passed it around. The joint passed me by two times before I decided to finally take a few hits. I cannot explain the feeling afterwards, perhaps I was dizzy or I might have gotten a headache. The next day Cheechee Marin heard that I had gotten high so he brought out a joint laced with hash oil. We smoked it and that time I definitely caught a buzz. From that day on, I always looked for a way to catch a buzz either with alcohol or drugs. That behavior turned into a lifestyle. That was a fork in the road of my life once I hit eighth grade. The pull between good and evil was reaching out to grab me. God and all His good was trying to save me and the devil with his forces of darkness were trying to destroy me; I mean this quite literally. Over time my actions gravitated more towards darkness and wrongful living. Eventually, I would experience blackness so dark that you could feel it.

I thought I was a good Catholic going to mass every week and then to confession. It is amazing how going to church lulls one into a false sense of security. We think we are right with God just because we go to church or just because we might have a little bit of religion. There are a lot of religious people in the world today who think they are doing God's will when they hurt others or destroy property in the name of religion. Knowing God is not about any type of religion, knowing God is about having a personal relationship with him through Jesus Christ. There is so much more in life that God wants us to experience through him. The Bible says there is a way that seems right to a man, but its way is the way of death (Proverbs 14:2). The way that seems right is to believe if you are good enough, if you are religious enough, if you give enough, and if you do enough good works, you might make it to Heaven. The Devil laughs because he knows that formula does not work. If it did, Jesus would not have had to hang on a cross to bleed every drop of his blood to wash away our sins. The only way to be made right with God is to have our sins forgiven. To take the free gift of Jesus blood from the cross and to ask Him to use it to wash away our sins. This is a personal act that must take place in the life of every human being in order for them to be born "the second time."

As a teenager I did not know about Bible truths. I was fourteen years old and the friends that I chose were on a path to destruction, to an end resulting in futility. My own personal life spun into a downward cycle towards a pit of destruction, where I should have been killed many times. The events of wrong doing which I am about to share may be difficult for some to comprehend. I am not proud of the past, only thankful to God that He allowed me to go through so much, in order that I might eventually look up to Him for help. I hope what is shared in the rest of this book will be beneficial to those reading it.

My friends and I stumbled upon a treatment plant while looking for places to fish in the sloughs of the Wisconsin River. The treatment plant for the Appaloosa Paper Company was being constructed during 1975 and 1976. The building was going up, clarifiers were being built, and lagoons were being dug in the north west section of the Town of Saratoga. Many years later I would be hired as summer help to work at that plant, but as fifteen year olds we explored the area and sometimes found ourselves getting into trouble. It was at that time that I found out my companions were little thieves. The winter of 1975 and 1976 was an extremely cold one. For recreation we would go to Dave Mauer's house and then down below the hill to party on some land just west of Mandela's marsh. We would build large bon fires and ice skate out on the ponds. When our party was over, my 1.5 mile walk home was a cold one. That year the nights were over twenty degrees below zero. When a person breathed in through their nose, the insides of their nostrils would freeze shut. Spring arrived that next year as it always does and with it came thoughts of fishing and shooting carp with our bows. One March day we proceeded through the woods north of the old nursery road, to shoot carp back in the river sloughs east of the treatment plant. I was walking out on the ice toward the river when I encountered rotted ice and fell through. I was wearing chest waders and the water was so deep that the waders filled up; there was no way that I could get out by myself. Fortunately, the other guys were able to pull me out to safety. Were it not for them I would have died of hypothermia at the young age of fifteen, but God had other plans for me.

Cutting classes was a popular pastime for high school students in the 1970's. Paul had a large green car, possibly a Buick, so on nice days several of us would pile into his car and cruise out of town on excursions into the country. On one trip we found ourselves at Castle Rock down on highway 21 east of Necedah. On that day we realized Paul was not fit to drive after drinking only two beers. His car made it through Devil's Elbow but only after nearly missing the curves on the way back to school.

XMan was my roommate for over a decade.

I was in my bedroom one day and for some reason I was looking for something in XMan's top dresser drawer. A camouflaged piece of material caught my eye so I picked it up and looked at it. Inside the material was a small jar full of money, a lot of money. There were twenties, fifties and hundreds, literally thousands of dollars. There was so much money that I felt XMan would not miss any if I took a twenty to buy an ounce of weed. The next time it was easier to steal, then again and again until the money was mostly gone. Imagine little old me being so popular once I had that money. Of course none of the people who wanted to party were really my friends. Some dealers ripped me off just as I ripped off XMan; I deserved it, I had that coming. I guess I was either really dumb, or naïve to do what I did. For the next few years I thought that just going to church and confession would still make me a good person, but was I ever wrong! Obviously I was not paying attention to the commandment which says, "Thou shalt not steal" (Exodus 20:15). God is not mocked when we do wrong, eventually our sin finds us out. Harold McWhorter put it best when he said, "Sin will take you farther than you wanna go, slow but wholly taking control. Sin will leave you longer than you wanna stay, sin will cost you far more than you wanna pay."

Floyd Simpson had just joined the National Guards and was in boot camp. I decided to sit down and write him a letter. I started out my letter by swearing so that it would sound "cool." Then I talked about all of the drugs that were available here at home and all of the parties that were going on. Before I could mail it, Mom found the letter. I realized she had the letter because she knew things I had written about. I remember I wanted to go somewhere one day, so I went to ask for her permission. I talked to her through a closed door while she was in the bathroom. Mom then replied back to me by quoting the first sentence of my letter. At that point, I knew the game was up so I just played dumb. I didn't acknowledge I knew she had my letter. I just repeated my question to go over to my friend's house.

Mom did not yet know that I had been taking money. However, she did find out other incriminating information about my latest escapades because of the letter. In fact, I suspect that she may have been reading my letter that day when I knocked on the bathroom door, because Mom did not want to see me ruin my life. It was not long before she started talking to other mothers to find out what was going on between my friends and me. I believe there was even talk that she contacted the Wausau division of the FBI to try and stop the flow of drugs into my life. Mom did her best and like Merle Haggard said, "I was twenty one in prison doing life without parole, but momma tried, momma tried."

I began to feel uneasy after Mom read the letter. I felt like I was being watched. It was only two weeks later when the Sheriffs Deputies pulled up alongside of me on County trunk Z as I was walking on the shoulder of the road. I felt like an animal being stalked as they rolled to a stop and lowered their window on the squad car. I did not consider myself to be a drug dealer, but a drug user. It was never my intent to sell drugs. I merely hoped to make friends with people by keeping the party going. So I was on my way to Bart's house with a pound of marijuana in my army jacket as I casually made small talk with the officers. I played it cool until they drove off out of sight but I wondered if they would come back to see where I was going. Had they been tailing me? Did Mom put them on to me? I forced myself to leisurely walk a short ways up to the high lines and headed west for two hundred yards. Then I turned south and ran half a mile through the woods until I hit the dry run. I headed east toward Lester's property and walked to Strangeline Road. It was there that I stashed the dope in a culvert under the road. I was safe at last, or so I thought.

Prom night at school was a special time of friendships for some classmates, a time of boys spending time with girls, an evening of warm memories, but for me it was a day just like any other day. Those "special times" of intimacy were foreign to me. I had built up walls to protect myself and there was no way I would even consider going to a prom ceremony. That night in May, 1975 I met up with a few other teens out on the high lines west of Country Sports Center. At that time there were two major places where parties could be found: at the high lines or a place called Ho Chi, out by the yellow banks on Lake Petenwell. We were on the high lines waiting for news as to where the party was going to take place that night. We heard it was going to be at Ho Chi, so I scored a gram of hash oil, found a glass pipe, and away we went to Petenwell. Paul's car began having problems that night after the party was over, so we had to get a tow back to Appaloosa. It was pouring rain all the way back to town. The hour was late and I ended up staying the night at Paul's house along with five other partiers. At the house we all went upstairs and I was shocked at what happened next, an orgy. Here I was, a virgin sixteen year old wasted on hash oil. As the lights went out, Cindy taught us lessons too bizarre to ever forget. That evening was the first time that I had ever stayed away from home for an entire night without Mom's permission. I knew I was going to be in big trouble so instead of going home, I decided to go somewhere else.

Bart and I left Appaloosa at 5:30 A.M. and walked over four miles to Bumblebee's trailer over on Young Street. Once we were there, I scored three ounces of Mexican and still had fifty dollars in cash left over. Bird and Little Louie were doing opium in the next room and the rest of us were getting ready to start smoking weed. I happened to be looking out the living room window towards the driveway when my heart suddenly sank. The old Dodge Dart was pulling in with Mom and my siblings. Bart's mom must have called other parents when he did not come home the night before. My mind raced as I tried to figure out what to do. There was no way that I wanted to go home and get hassled. My adrenaline kicked in when that car appeared in the driveway and I tore out the back door of Bumblebee's trailer and stashed the money and pot out in the woods. Later, the other guys found the drugs and cash and kept it for themselves. Meanwhile, my mom made it known that she was not about to leave without me, so the guys called me to come back from the woods. As I walked back to the trailer, I wondered out loud why I was even going back home. I reluctantly walked up to the car, hopped in, and rode home in silence.

Looking back to forty years ago, I am sad at what I must have put my mom through. She really did love each of her children and must have laid awake all night wondering where I was. She must have wondered whether I was hurt or even alive. Today I would be upset if one of my children or grandchildren would show up missing overnight without an explanation as to why. Once we arrived home it was confession time. I confessed to taking money out of the dresser drawer, but was I sorry? No. I was not! After that day, I continued stealing money. I picked locked boxes and even raided the cash in my dad's closet. I did not care about the consequences. I just wanted drugs!

The day after Mom pulled me out of Bumblebee's trailer was Monday and time to go back to school. It was a beautiful spring morning and I was supposed to cut class with the others. They were going to cruise out past Babcock, but I decided to stay in class that day. The last thing I wanted was to get in any more trouble, at least not for a while. Paul left the school parking lot with a full car and headed towards Babcock. They traveled through town and came to the Yellow River. I found out later that some-one came up with the bright idea to go swimming. Bart decided to be the first to dive into the water. The only problem was the water was only two feet deep so when Bart dove in, he hit his head on a rock. He came up out of the water with a nasty gash on his head, blood streaming down his face. Everyone freaked out because they did not want to get in trou-ble by taking Bart to the hospital. Paul decided the best thing to do was to rush to Appaloosa to see a doctor, but Paul was in no condition to drive. He lost control while driving the car at ninety miles per hour on the curve east of Hemlock Creek. The vehicle flew off of the road and ended up rolling many times. The car was totaled and it was a miracle that no one was killed. For once I was glad that I did the right thing by staying in school that day.

Summer arrived and Mom began trying to figure out how to get me back on the straight and narrow path of life. She felt the only way for me to change and do good was for me to be removed from the influence of my friends. That summer, I ended up working on my great uncle's dairy farm southwest of Marshfield on Highway 10, just down the hill from Nasonville. I made sure to plant some pot seeds on Lester Smart's land before I left for the dairy farm. It is important to remember that there has to be inward change in a person's heart for that person to want to change their lifestyle. For me, there was yet no change in my circumstances at home with my parents. Yes, I had shelter, food, and clothes on my back, but I wanted more. I had no one to spend time with, so I continued escaping life with drugs and alcohol. Up at my uncle's farm, I found moonshine and was able to buy six packs of beer from the tavern on top of the hill. And when I arrived back home a month later my marijuana was big enough to pull, dry, and smoke.

11

Chapter Eleven

Drugs, Drugs and More Drugs

Bert Pepowski grew up in Portage County and eventually became a priest. As a Catholic missionary from Green Bay, he held a week of meetings at Sacred Heart Catholic church during the Lenten season of 1977. Father Bert shared about the possibility of every Catholic having a personal relationship with Jesus Christ, along with a fullness of the gifts of the Holy Spirit. This was during a time of charismatic renewal among the mainline denominations all across America. The phenomenon made its way into the Catholic Church during the mid-1960s. Participants in the charismatic movement believed not only in the sacraments and church doctrine of the Roman Catholic Church, but they believed much more. They believed that the gifts of the Holy Spirit did not die out with the Apostles and that those gifts were still available for believers and followers of Jesus today. People in the charismatic movement also realized that it was possible to be born again and have a daily personal relationship with Jesus Christ.

My dad attended all of the services throughout

the week that were offered by Father Bert. On one Wednesday evening service he was deeply affected. Dad cried all the way home that night but he did not know why. However, he felt deep down that he had failed miserably in life. Once Dad arrived home, he tried to talk to Mom about the teachings that he had heard about at church. She wanted nothing to do with it. The die was cast and the events she planned were about to take their course.

Mom made her move and left Dad for good on May 27, 1977. She took my siblings and left the area to reside in another part of the state and I went to stay with a relative named Ralph in Schaumburg, Illinois, a suburb of Chicago. Dad was devastated at the loss of his family and described his overwhelming loss in public testimonies both at church and at Full Gospel Business Association meetings. The agony Dad endured is best described in one of his speeches from 1989 as quoted from the following excerpts:

> "I came home one night, my family was gone and most of the furniture; there was a note saying 'David I don't love you anymore, don't try to find us.' That was the biggest shock I have ever had in my whole life. I literally got sick and my stomach was upset for months. I tried to find them for about three months until one night at the kitchen table I was talking to God and crying and

I got this distinct message – give them up! Now, even though I did not know much about salvation, I wanted to do things God's way, so from that night on, I quit looking for them and I did not see them until about nine months later in divorce court. I was told I did not have any visiting rights. So I did not have any family, and I quit that foolishness of trying to make a lot of money, so I had a lot of time on my hands. I put that time to good use by going to Bible studies and different spiritual speakers and looking for a church that was alive..."

Dad eventually had an experience with Jesus. From that time onward he prayed that I would come back to him.

I worked as a seventeen year old common laborer in the condo building industry that summer after the break - up. I was told it was my responsibility to work hard, keep my nose clean, and "straighten up." What a joke! On my first day of work all of the trim carpenters told me what a lush Ralph was, and to make matters worse, he kept a stash of reefer for his own personal use. Then there was the matter of his porn magazines and the fights with his girlfriend.

There was no running away from drugs, they were readily available everywhere I went and the possibility of getting arrested. As a matter of fact,

I was nearly busted in Chicagoland. The guys I was hanging out with had some Columbian gold, so we smoked some and then gave each other wall hits. A wall hit is where you hold the smoke in your lungs, and as you do so, someone from behind gives you a bear hug. This intensifies the rush. We were pretty wasted and started bumping cars. As we did, their car alarms went off. We headed towards our garage at the condo, and soon some older boys showed up with three ounces of pot. Now we were going to have a real party. Someone began separating seeds out of the buds and the seeds were falling onto the floor while someone else was getting ready to roll joints. Suddenly, three squad cars pulled up to the entrance of the garage and cops were scrambling to get out of their cars. Apparently, the owners of the vehicles had called the cops. We quickly kicked seeds and bags of weed under the car before the officers could get to our side of the vehicle. A piercing code three then came over their car radios and the cops took off with lights flashing and tires spinning. Another disaster averted where I did not get busted. How lucky can a person get?

August arrived and with it came thoughts of finishing high school; those thoughts turned my stomach. I did not want to go to a school with thousands of people I did not know. I would have loved to have gone back to school in Appaloosa, but that was not an option for me. My mom had moved away, and I did not trust Dad. How could I trust someone that I did not know? For all of the crud that happened in my school years, there was also some good. There were people that I was able to get along with in school that I really liked. Looking back, I wish I could have been a part of their lives.

One day, Dad called me on the phone while I was still living in Schaumburg. He was blubbering and telling me how lonely he was, and how badly he wanted me home with him. Well I was lonely, too. In fact, I had been lonely for seventeen years! There was never a bond, never a father and son talk. I remember trying to speak to Dad once when I was twelve years old. He was getting ready to go down into the new well to haul out more sand. He cut me off as soon as I began talking to him and told me to "stop my prattle." Well as far as I was concerned, Dad could kiss my grits. As our phone conversation ended, Dad said that he was going to come down to Schaumberg to visit me. I knew that he would persuade me to come home, so I snuck away to Carthage, Wisconsin before he could arrive.

Carthage, what a dope town that turned out to be. Not far away was a methamphetamine or speed manufacturing lab out in the country with six to seven million dollars' worth of product. Scattered throughout the surrounding county were also small pot plantations. The area was relatively close to Madison or "Mad" town, so you could get nearly any drug that you wanted. In 1977, the methamphetamine lab was busted and its negative influence on the community was done away with. Carthage today is a wonderful mecca of opportunity, second to none. Surrounded by amazing natural beauty and limitless business opportunities, it is a place everyone should visit and check out as a place to live. Law enforcement has done an outstanding job in the last thirty eight years in making Carthage a wholesome clean community where people feel safe and secure, but it was very different when I stayed there in 1977.

I arrived in Carthage in August of 1977 and toured the town on the very first day of my arrival. My first observation was of a red log cabin shelter house in a park. In the background was a dike to keep the river in its banks during flood stage. It was in that park that car loads of youth and young adults partied or met to look for parties. It seemed as though everyone was preoccupied with finding drugs, drugs, and more drugs.

My first job in Carthage was at a Deep Rock Gas Station and I was trained by a fella named Gordy Whitemarsh. There were opportunities at the station but after a week, I left. The locking up at night made me nervous and I was worried that I might forget a task at closing time. The station manager really did not want to lose me as an employee, but I felt inadequate. I did not want to deal with the possibility of failure. The next week I began attending Frederick Douglas High School. Not knowing a soul but Gordy, I felt alienated and out of place. That November, I turned 18 and dropped out of school. I know it broke Mom's heart and grieved my grandparents but I just couldn't finish. Wandering in town one afternoon, I noticed an Army recruiting office. I stepped in to check it out. It turns out they only wanted recruits with a high school diploma, so I had no other option except to find a job.

The next week I found work in the cheese industry at AMPI milk producers as a fork lift operator. Six weeks on the job, they relocated me to the cooking plant. The environment was wet and humid. This caused my skin to itch and created red blotches from head to toe. I quit at the end of the day. Later on, I found out the manager in that plant did not want to lose me as an employee and would have been willing to relocate me in the plant. Finding another job was easy because in the late 1970's, there seemed to be an endless supply of jobs in that town. The next company that I worked for was Carthage Industries. My job was once again to be a fork lift operator and a third hand on a plastics extrusion machine. Carthage Industries had thermoform molds for over 140 different products made out of plastic. We manufactured dashes for Ford Motor Company, tractor cabs, tub surrounds, bed pans... I did well in that company and stayed several months until one night I saw Dad's truck in town. Mom didn't want him near us so she moved us all to Blackhawk, Wisconsin.

Drugs were at the center of my life while I was a teenager. I did drugs while I attended high school and when I worked at the gas station, cheese plant, and plastics factory. The one goal of my friends was to get high, even into old age, and to smoke joints with their grandchildren. Their motto was, "With booze you lose but with dope there's hope." The people I hung out with were hard core drug users. I do not know all the kinds of drugs we took as there were so many of them: white cross speed, green and clears, Quaalude 714s commonly called horse tranquilizers, hash, hash oil, Thai stick, peyote, blotter acid, purple micro dot. There was also the meth lab outside of town. Who knows what you were ingesting from that place. I remember when you dropped the white tablets from there into a bottle of Mountain Dew, the pop would practically fizzle up into the bottle neck.

I sowed all of my wild oats from the ages of fifteen to nineteen, and in that same time, I wasted around ten thousand dollars on substance abuse. It's funny, but before I began taking drugs, my friends would tell me, "Don't knock it unless you try it." I have been drug free for thirty six years. In that time I have been anti-drug all of the way, and yes, I have the right to knock drugs because I tried drugs. People in many states want recreational use of marijuana legalized but I believe that line of thinking is wrong. I have been totally opposed to drugs ever since March 4, 1979. No one can call me a square or say don't knock it until you've tried it. I tried it, and not only did drugs mess up my life, but I watched it mess up the lives of many other people.

The drug world was often brutal to those associated with it. I remember one day we went to Jay's house to get some pot and a drug dealer by the name of Jason was there. I had never met the guy before and he had never met me. The guy took a gun out of his belt, showed me the loaded cylinders and stuck the barrel right over my heart and tight onto my chest. Jason proceeded to pull the hammer back and with a nasty look on his face said, "If you're a narc I'm going to blow you away." I smiled and said, "Go ahead." Another incident revolved around a fellow named Neil. He was from the area of Rio, south east of Carthage. His nickname was the Jack Pine Savage." One day a group of us went with Neil to help harvest his pot plantation. I call it a plantation because there were hundreds of plants. We pulled the cannabis, separated male from female, and then bundled, tied, and hung the plants upside down so all of the chemical agents from the roots would migrate into the leaves. Neil did not talk much and if he did not like you, then look out. He had a very stocky build and cops had their hands full when they would try and take this guy down. He had coal black hair and his sparse black mustache looked a lot like Charles Bronson's. One night Neil and his buddies decided they were going to beat the crap out of Heike Davis, a former marine who was always bragging how tough he was. They also had it in for a long hair from Lodi by the name of Nelson Richter. On that night those two unfortunate fellas had many missing teeth and bloody faces. It pays not to mess with some people.

Brutality was not reserved just for people. Quite often it was reserved for property. One night four of us guys were bored, so we went to a car dealership and tipped over a car on the car lot. On another night, we found out Curtiss could not make the payments on his car, so Brian Wilson stole the keys and said to me, "Let's take a ride." What he didn't share with me was he planned to steal the car and "total" it so Curtiss could collect on the insurance. Brian drove through the streets of Carthage at ninety miles per hour going to the north and then he did the same thing going to the south. He ran every stop sign and traffic light that he came to. The climax of our little trip was when Brian drove the car into a swamp just outside of town at fifty miles per hour. The finale was when he finished off the car by kicking out the windows, real bright! Incidentally, the insurance investigator for the car lived just across the street from Curtiss. Needless to say, there was no payout.

I remember another incident when it was snowing very hard, so Brian decided it was the perfect time to rip off a gas company. It was located back behind Ray O Vac. He siphoned gas and stole cases of oil then he senselessly ripped a company radio out of a truck, which he threw into the Carthage canal. The next day Brian and I were walking on the east side of town. We noticed a beer truck parked in front of a warehouse with the side doors rolled open. The driver went into the building so Brian grabbed six packs of Pabst Blue Ribbon and away we ran.

Drugs can also be brutal on the human body. One night I was standing in the park. I just had a couple of beers then I smoked a joint and snorted butyl nitrite. I passed out and fell into a mud puddle while I was talking to some people in a car. Afterwards, I walked toward home and made it four blocks before I passed out again. I woke up to the sight of a cop shining his spotlight on me from his squad car. He asked me if I had enough to drink. I said, "No," got myself up off the ground, and walked the rest of the way home. On another night I was in our home at the trailer park. My sisters were watching television in the living room while I sat in my bedroom and drank a bottle of Yukon Jack. I passed out on the bathroom floor for a while, but when I woke up, I went to the park, found some friends, drove north to Mason Lake by Briggsville, and partied all night.

Another point I want to make, is that dope makes you a lawbreaker in the worst way. It gives you the "who cares" attitude of apathy towards everything that one should hold important and dear. God, family, values... it makes you lukewarm and it totally obliterates your convictions. I know half of society wants to defend drug use but I feel their views are baseless. I made good with the police thirty six years ago when I was still a teenager. I have lumped together these events which took place in Carthage, Blackhawk and Dover during a fourteen month time period. These events were all drug related behaviors that people would not usually do if they were not on drugs. Lawlessness was so rampant in our '70s drug culture. I think it would be an understatement to say some youth acted as though they were members to a crime of the month club.

The epitome of stupidity happened on Good Friday 1978. I really should have been in church on that day with my mother and sisters, but I wasn't. What faith I did have in my far away God must have been awful shallow. I would suspect that I did not even know what day of the month it was at the time, much less that it was one of the most important holy days of the year. Isn't it funny how we deceive ourselves into thinking that we are not so bad when in reality we are? On that Friday, Carthage was dry, I mean, no one had any drugs. I suggested to Brian that we make a trip to Appaloosa, and score some drugs from my former classmates. We hooked up with Mike and Ramsey at the Gate 5 tavern, but they had nothing, so we all decided to go to Kings Knight in Grand Rapids. At Kings Knight we scored an ounce of pot and bought a case of beer, which we stuck in the back window. We were so wasted that we did not know what we were doing. The driver of our car backed up in the parking lot and hit a brand new Camaro. Well, we never felt the vehicles hit so we took off. Little did we know that an APB went out on police radios throughout the state to apprehend our vehicle for hit and run.

We drove back to Appaloosa and dropped off Mike and Ramsey and then we started out on our trip back to Carthage. We were at the stop sign and turning right to go across the Wisconsin River Bridge when we heard the siren and saw the flashing lights behind us. Officer "Bud" Moody, my former Boy Scout master, stepped out of the squad car and asked us if we knew that we hit a car in Grand Rapids. He said, "I'm going to have to take you boys in," so we took a ride in the squad car to the Wood County courthouse. During the trip, Officer Bud and I talked about old times and he assured me that I was basically a good kid. The driver of our car ended up spending the night in jail. My other friend and I began hitchhiking to Carthage at 11:00 P.M. that night. A motorist picked us up as we were walking along Eighth Street. It was Bill Hohenstein. Bill lived on Highway 13 just south of Ranger Road and offered to let us spend the night at his house. The next morning after we woke up, Bill put some cultic Bahai music on the phonograph and asked me how I liked it. I said that it did nothing for me so we left and hitched rides back to Carthage.

With drugs you make irrational decisions and have all kinds of bizarre ideas. Appaloosa Paper workers used to have mill strikes when they felt that management was being unfair to them during bargaining sessions. During one of those strikes, I remember one night tripping out on purple microdot with Paul. The two of us stood by Market Street staring at the mill. Paul's whole focus was on the gigantic building. Minutes ticked by until Paul finally spoke. His profound thought for the night was that the world would collapse economically if the mill ever shut down.

I was living in Carthage and I was still going to church off and on. I thought my life was ok and that I had it all together, but I was deluded. Christmas season came and with it the manger scene on the main street of Carthage. The nativity scene was lit up at night, with scenes of tranquility and peace on earth, so what did I do? I kicked out the flood lights. You know, people say that we are all children of God. A more accurate statement is that we all belong to the brotherhood of man. As far as God is concerned, we are not His children until we come to the cross and are spiritually born into His Kingdom. It is only through the blood of Jesus on the cross that our personal sins can be washed away (Romans 5:6 -11; 1 Peter 1:18 – 21). The apostle Paul while writing to the Galatian believers said the following in Galatians 3:36, "So in Christ Jesus you are all children of God through faith." I had not yet come to God through faith in Christ Jesus. I was trying to come to God through religion. So here I was, a lost sinner, living in darkness and doing works of darkness. The apostle John makes it very clear on what it means to be born of God as we see in John 1:12, 13, "Yet to all who received him, to those who believed in his name, he gave the right to become children of God – children born not of natural descent, nor of human decision or a husband's will, but born of God."

I have heard people tell me that when they get high they have better concentration doing school work, or, that they work better on the job. I do not believe that people are in the mood to work when they get high, either that, or drugs are not as potent as they were in the 70s. The expression "getting stoned," was coined for a reason. You just sat there like a rock, oblivious to what was going on around you. There was no concept of time and you did not know whether your feet were up in the air or down on the ground. You were basically able to "take a trip without leaving the farm." Life in the 70s really was like a Cheech and Chong movie.

On December 4, 1977 between the time that I worked at the cheese factory and the plastics factory, Vander Stanleyhoff and I decided that we were going to hitch hike to California. At noon on that day, I gathered my clothes together and then went down town for a snowball fight with my friends. As I walked past a gas station, I noticed a station wagon with the windows all fogged up. A guy rolled down his window and asked me if I wanted to smoke some Thai stick so I said sure and started toking. I found out the people in the wagon were from Montello, a town half an hour to the north, and they were in town to play a concert for the local junior high school. Later, I went back home, ate, showered and then headed over to the gas station again. I thought that I was ready to go to California. I had no money, three cans of vegetable soup, a can of spaghetti, a duffel bag full of clothes, and a .410 shotgun. What was I planning to do with a .410 shotgun, protect myself? When Vander arrived he had two duffel bags stuffed full of clothes. The bags must have weighed 50 pounds apiece. He had packed so it was not long before his expensive clothes ended up in the ditch; talk about dumb and dumber, we were it!

Brian Wilson drove the two us to the intersection of Highway 51 and 16 and dropped us off. It was 6:00 P.M. The night was frigid and the snow began falling hard with the wind periodically whipping, swirling the snow into dust devils. Traffic began to slow as one lane of the highway began drifting over. Here we were, a couple of losers starting a trip in the darkness during a snow storm and our only plan was we were hitchhiking all of the way. We walked alongside the road for a couple of miles hauling our bags up and down the rolling hills until an old man with a boy on their way to Poynette picked us up. After they dropped us off, the next ride took us another twenty miles to a Mad Town truck stop where Highway 151 crosses Highway 51. It was midnight as we stood knee deep in snow waiting for a ride. It was a long cold wait until a van load of partiers picked us up and drove us south towards Janesville. I do not remember too much from that point on, except that the driver let us crash overnight at his pad. The next day we hitched a ride south to an area north of Rockford and then found another ride that took us 55 miles east. We were only 6 miles from Vander's brother's house in Antioch so we spent the night there. All of the walking tired us out so we decided not to go to California after all. The next day I hitched all the way back to Carthage by myself. How could two 18 year olds make so many dumb decisions? The answer is drugs. Drug abuse was rampant back then, a lifestyle for many.

12

Chapter Twelve

God Works in Mysterious ways

Dad had been looking for us for months. He missed his family more than words could say. One Saturday evening in May, 1978, I went to evening mass with my mother and my siblings. We were looking for an open spot to park the car when I spotted Dad's truck. Mom panicked, so we drove 120 miles to her parents that night. Dad had not yet learned that he could not force situations to change, he needed to learn to sit back and wait on God to make things happen. A few weeks later we all moved to Blackhawk.

During this time, God was busy though. He heard Dad's prayers from the very first day that we left him. God was even working on my heart without me knowing it. It's funny how God helps us when we cry out to him, as He works all situations into His perfect plan. Time after time we continue to walk out of His will as we do our own thing. Yet He continues to craft new ways to draw us back towards him. We must give God time to change not only us, but also situations and people surrounding us.

I know it sounds funny, but in those lonely months without his family, Dad found Jesus. You see, it was Dad who was lost. Dad was looking for the truth about life, and as he searched for answers he found God. God tells us in Jeremiah 29:13, "You will seek me and find me, when you seek me with all your heart." This means much more than going to church or just being religious. By reaching out to God and seeking a deeper understanding and loving relationship with him, Dad became a witness to Christ's words in John 15:5 "I am the vine; you are the branches. If you remain in me and I in you, you will bear much fruit; apart from me you can do nothing." Dad discovered that God desires a personal relationship with him just as he desires a personal relationship with every human being ever created.

Unbeknown to me, Dad and his friends were praying for me. For over a year while I was living in Chicagoland, Carthage and Blackhawk, they would meet on Sunday nights in the basement of Sacred Heart Catholic church. Those charismatic born again Catholics were singing to Jesus and praying to Jesus. With their hands humbly raised to heaven in total surrender they prayed for me: My father, big John Cattanach, Jim Mason, Lucy Rose Johns and her parents, Jane Martinson, George and Rita Carlson, Frank and Betty Raab, Norman and Florence Heil, Father Wilger, Donna Fekete... In heaven I will thank them someday.

I arrived in Blackhawk with my mom and

family in June and back in Appaloosa that summer those dear Catholics kept praying. Throughout the hot months I was extremely restless. Out of the clear blue I took off one weekend and hitch hiked back to Carthage to spend time at Stanleyhoffs. On another weekend, I actually began riding my bicycle to Appaloosa to see my dad, but after fifteen miles I became tired and turned back towards Blackhawk. It's hard to believe, but I think the prayers of other people were drawing and pulling me back towards Appaloosa. It was as though I were a piece of metal being pulled towards a magnet. Dad did not have to do anything but pray, while God began a stirring in my heart - unreal!

In Blackhawk I partied less than I did in Carthage because I did not know many people, but drugs were still available. One day Benny Sandstone and Navid Steller came from Carthage to visit my siblings and to party. I was invited along for the ride so I bought a six pack of beer. We ended up driving to a park but we unknowingly parked in a restricted area. No sooner had we cut the engine when a squad car pulled in behind us. We tried stashing everything under the seats but the officers knew what we were doing. They said, "Everyone out of the car," so we left the vehicle and stood in a line. Next, they told everyone to give their ages, so each of us spoke up when it was our turn: 14, 15, 16, and 16. When I said 18, the cop said bingo! I was scared and did not want to go to jail. I was a stupid little punk! Navid ended up telling the officer that it was his pot. After the officers took down our names we were allowed to go.

Not having a high school diploma, I was forced to work temporary manual labor jobs. In Blackhawk we lived north of Pittman field where the FAA took place each summer. We were in a trailer park just east of Packer Pub Bar and only a mile from Highway 41, so I rode my bike to work each day. I was employed by Jay's Manufacturing company, and it was my job to grind welds on fenders and then to dip them in a de oiling solution. The fenders were made for vehicles being built by Blackhawk trucking. This job lasted for just the summer. Our next residence was Dover Pine village. The first job I had in Dover that August was at the trailer park. My job was to dig large holes by hand for installation of new septic tanks. With the help of another fellow, we also spread dump truck loads of dirt for new lawns and built cement pads for storage sheds and new trailer houses. I'm sure our physical labors saved the park director thousands of dollars by not having to outsource a backhoe. The next job I applied for was at Steel King as a fork lift operator. My responsibility was to truck loose steel tubes in a pallet cradle. I only stayed there for a few days because the close quarters between the forklift lanes were too close to the workers doing welding. It made me nervous to think that someone might get hurt if I made one wrong move with the forklift.

Eventually I realized the importance of having a high school diploma, so on October 24, 1978 I walked into a college at University of Wisconsin Stevens Point, took a GED test, and passed. I now had a diploma but without a driver license my employment options were still rather limited. Why didn't I just go get a driver license? Well the answer is that I was too nervous to ride with a driver's license examiner because I was afraid of failure. Deep down I had low self-esteem and was too chicken to get a driver's license. Also, doing drugs made me very short sighted; they kept me from seeing the big picture of life. I saw no future for myself at all. No dreams, no goals, and no direction in life.

I was introduced to a guy by the name of Bob who lived in a small trailer park by the intersection of Highway 54 and County Road B in Dover. The park was across from Adams Family Towing service. On one particular day, Bob and I started drinking at his trailer beginning in the afternoon. By suppertime we were doing blotter acid. When I did certain types of drugs an awareness would awaken within me and that day was no different. Only a person who did drugs would understand what I am talking about. There is a realization of life from a totally different perspective than that of someone who does no drugs. I would look into the mirror, and it was as though my soul inside my body was looking out into the mirror, and I could look back into myself. I know what I am saying sounds bizarre, but you can be perfectly sober and look into a mirror up close and actually see the reflection of your face in your pupils staring back at you.

Matthew 6:22 says "The eye is the lamp of the body; so then if your eye is clear, your whole body will be full of light. But if your eye is bad, your whole body will be full of darkness. If then the light that is in you is darkness, how great is the darkness!" So there I was in the trailer with this guy Bob and his wife, drinking, doing acid, and playing poker. As the night went on, I found myself looking into Bob's eyes, and the more I looked into those dark pools, the louder an inner voice said there was something dark in those eyes! What happened next was embarrassing. I was so full from drinking beer that when I took a pull from the can I could not swallow, I just spit it out. The owner of the trailer was furious and he told me to get out!

The walk home was about a mile. It was late and the night was satanically black. The eerie shadows of trees shuddered and jerked across the roadway. I was in the fifth dimension beyond sight and sound. Feeling what I saw and felt, I wondered what happens to you the instant you die. Does God snatch you up and take you to Him, or does the devil and his shadowy host lie in wait, hoping for an ambush, to drag you off to hell. My question to my mother from when I was twelve years old had never been answered.

I did not know it, but my life was about to rapidly sink lower. The night in the dark was part of a battle between God and Satan for my soul. I know that Mom prayed for me as best as she could, and

Dad with all of his prayer friends were pounding heaven with their prayers. God and his angels were fighting on my behalf; meanwhile, Satan and his demonic agents of evil were trying to keep me in their grasp.

Mom began looking at properties for a house in a more permanent location. There was a property west of Dover owned by a fellow named Don. Don seemed like a nice enough guy so I hung out with him and his buddies. The group was like a network of criminals or scammers. Some of them were thieves and ex-cons, and like myself they figured the "system" was corrupt. Of course there was nothing wrong with them; it was society that was messed up. Many of those guys were out of work like I was, so they drank, smoked pot and played cribbage. Don, Kevin, Ray, Bob, Kenny and Ken were so hard up for money, that they taught me how to play cribbage; just so they could make a penny a point off of me.

The final curtain call was about to begin just before my spiritual birth. Don had been busted for allegedly driving after revocation one night out by Arnott or Polonia, and for running into the back of another car. I am not sure if he fled the scene or what happened because the next day he offered me a hundred dollars to say that I was driving the car. Don was twenty seven and I was eighteen. So here he is with the bright idea to bribe me into taking the witness stand during a jury trial in court. I was to say that I drove the vehicle during the hit and run. What was that guy thinking? I did not even have a driver's license. I would have been busted for the hit and run and I was not even at the scene of the crime. This selfish guy did not care about what would happen to me, all he cared about was saving his own butt. I must have had stupid written all over my face to have said yes to Don. Was it because he was my only friend at the time? In my stupidity I gave no thought to the consequences of perjuring myself on the witness stand. I did not even know what perjury was so I went to court and lied on the witness stand for Don.

I suppose lying on the witness stand was like selling my soul to the devil; obviously I no longer had anything resembling a conscience. Here I was thinking my life was ok, but in all reality the law was going to come after me for the many crimes that I knew about. My association with criminals and perjuring myself on the witness stand; perhaps I could have ended up in prison. I was oblivious to those facts. Looking back, I just cannot believe that I raised my hand, and swore on the Bible, to tell the whole truth and nothing but the truth.

They say that you can never pull the wool over your mother's eyes. In the case of my mother that was true. Mom knew that I was up to no good by the company that I kept. She did not know exactly what I had been doing but those late hours away from home could only mean trouble. Momma tried to get me to straighten up, she begged, yes begged and pleaded, for me to turn myself in to the authorities and to make restitution. I shrugged it all off. I thought I was "all right." I mean, I did not kill anybody did I?

Dad was still praying with his charismatic friends in the Catholic Church every Sunday night. I am not talking about repetitious prayers out of a missalette, I am talking about petitioning God the Father in Jesus' name. Passionate prayers from their hearts to God. I did not know what Dad was doing as I unknowingly kept digging my hole deeper and deeper. A hole so deep, that I would not be able to get out of it by myself. Burglaries were happening all around Dover and throughout the state. Don was wanted for illegal activities in Buffalo County and soon his actions would complicate my life. Stolen guns were being sold like burgers at the county fair by one of my ex con friends. I even happened to be walking around with one of the hand guns. It never occurred to me that the gun was hot, I did not even have shells for the gun. I only wore a gun because it made me feel like I was someone bigger, and better than I knew I was. It was a conversation piece to make me feel important.

God had things under control, and He knew that He would straighten my life out, if I made but one right choice. Like I said, Dad was praying, and God had planned an appointment for me to attend. First I had to take the bait so I could be reeled in. You know, God never wastes an experience, He can use all situations for His glory. He even uses our wrong motives, thoughts and desires to bring us to Him. My mind kept turning back to Appaloosa. What were the people doing that I once knew? I still remembered Dad as a crabby sucker. I really did not want anything to do with him, but I did want his money. I remembered that he used to keep a can of money up in his closet and I wondered if it was still there. Could I get into his house while he was gone? Maybe I could get some money and leave an I. O. U.

I hitch hiked from Dover to Strangeline Road and went to Dad's house. I quickly left with money in my pocket and went to a bar called Early America in Appaloosa. That night I was trying to impress everyone. I was acting like a jerk while Babe Ruth was sitting near me. I ended up hitting my beer glass into someone else's, and that is when Anthony Floss walked up to me. He told me to leave so I went outside for a while. Later I walked back into the bar. Anthony asked me why I came back into the bar as he was preparing to tear me apart. That was when Babe Ruth stood up and asked Anthony not to punch me out. Thank you Babe. What is really ironic, is how Babe was the ringleader of the CCD mob that once chased me down in the dark to beat me up over two years earlier. So Babe saved my sorry hide that night in the bar. Afterwards, Rodney Hermit stood up and offered to drive me all the way back home to Dover. I really did not know Rodney that well, but in looking back I sure am grateful that someone was watching over me.

It was snowing very hard the next week as I paced like a wild animal, back and forth on the south side of XMan's garage. I wanted to get into Dad's house for more money, but today his truck was in the driveway. What should I do? I never had a conversation with my dad in eighteen years, so what would I say to him now if he opened the door? My desire for drugs was greater than my fear of Dad, so I knocked on his door.

Steven Bornbach

13

Chapter Thirteen

A new creation

After nearly two years I had run full circle like a rabbit being chased by a hound, back to where I had started from. I had left a home without a relationship with my father. I was obviously still taking money, and I was still on drugs. Nothing had changed in my life during that time. Dad however had changed. I knocked on the door to his house and he was glad to see my face as he opened it; that seemed like a first. I entered into the house and we sat at his kitchen table. We actually had a conversation together, another first. The topic of our conversation did not interest me but I listened anyway, hoping that maybe I could leave with more money once Dad was all talked out.

Our conversation did not center on the topic of church. I did not hear about religion or about being religious. What Dad did talk about was the encounter he had with a person who died two thousand years ago. A man named Jesus Christ who rose from the dead and who is very much alive today. This idea of encountering Christ was something new to me. I had always thought of Jesus as being far, far, away, watching everything from Heaven. I saw artistic pictures of him in my CCD catechism and I read prayers to Him from a missalette. However, the missalette did not help me to know God and his word in a deep and meaningful way.

Sitting at the table, Dad began giving me his testimony. Prior to the family breakup during the charismatic renewal, Dad had begun searching for meaning in his life. Dad traveled everywhere around Wisconsin and neighboring states in search of truth about this life. One night he ended up at a Lowell Lundstrum crusade in LaCrosse, Wisconsin. The evangelist said anyone wanting to receive Christ should come up front by the altar for prayer. Dad ran forward without any hesitation. By the end of the night, there was no doubt in his mind that he had encountered Jesus. He was born again.

At the table Dad described the work that God did in his heart. The words he shared with me were much like the words he later spoke in his testimony during a church service. Here is an excerpt from that testimony:

> "I am David Bornbach and I have trusted Jesus as my Lord and Savior for about twelve years now. I still am not where I would like to be but at least I am willing to let God use me and I try to be open to what He wants me to do. I have the cer-

tain assurance and the peace in my heart
that even though I am not perfect I will
be in heaven someday. I have learned to
trust God in different ways, by reading
the Bible; by praying; by having people
pray for me..."

I quietly listened to Dad speak. There was a
change in his life and in his attitude. I was skeptical,
however, about the things that he was saying. Yet,
here Dad was friendly, talkative, and peaceful as he
shared his new found faith to me. He shared with
confidence and certainty. After listening patiently to
Dad for half an hour, I began to fidget and squirm
with impatience. So I changed the subject to that of
getting a car. What Dad found was fine for him but I
was not yet ready for what he had.

I asked Dad for money to buy a 1970 Gran Torino with a 351 Windsor. Dad agreed and handed me
five hundred dollars in cash. My shyster friend Don
who owned a junkyard west of Dover had offered
to sell me a Torino that was parked in his back yard.
What I had not told Dad, was that 1970 Gran Torino
was sitting without an engine. Don and I had agreed
when I came up with the money, he would drop an
engine into the car. In the end, Don had no ambi-
tion to drop in that engine, so I did not buy the car.
Instead, I spent the money on beer and drugs. Dad
had given me the money in good faith and I serious-
ly wanted to buy a car, but the impulse to party got
the best of me. The money quickly disappeared, so I

came up with another plan to get more cash.

A few days later I went back to Dad, but this time my purpose was to scam him out of his money. I had cooked up an outright lie. I was going to tell him that I needed more money to insure the car that I never really bought. Once again, I made the trip, hitching rides to Dad's house, and once again, he was home. Dad told me more about his new life in Jesus and he told me about a Sunday night praise and prayer group at the Catholic church. At the end of our visit, I told Dad that I needed another five hundred dollars to put insurance on the car I never bought. Dad gave me money on the condition that I go to a praise and prayer meeting with him on the next Sunday night. I reluctantly agreed. What I realize now is Dad was not stupid. Dad knew that it did not cost five hundred dollars to put insurance on an old car, but he felt that my soul was worth any amount of money. His faith in Jesus was so strong that he trusted God for a good outcome in my life. Let me say it again, his faith in Jesus was so strong.

God had a plan for my life. An appointed time where I was to be in his presence with others who had decided to become his children. You see it is a conscious decision to follow Christ. This is illustrated in the book of Mark 1:16 – 18: "As He was going along by the Sea of Galilee, He saw Simon and Andrew, the brother of Simon, casting a net in the sea; for they were fishermen. And Jesus said to them, "Follow me and I will make you fishers of men..." All throughout the New Testament mankind was exhorted as individuals to follow Jesus every day of their lives. The same holds true today.

The day for the Sunday praise and prayer meeting arrived. I remember the ride with Dad from his house to the church. I was nervous. No, actually, I was scared because I did not know what to expect. I suddenly wanted to back out and I told Dad so. His reply was "We are almost there." Dad always had to be half an hour early everywhere that he went. We were the first to arrive, so we sat down in the basement waiting for each person to enter the room. Of course, I had to be introduced to each person who walked through the door and I had to be polite and make small talk with them. I was climbing the walls! Every person told me that God loved me and each person gave me a hug. Little old ladies and even the men gave me hugs.

I was a long haired druggy. Why was everyone going out of their way to be so kind to me? Why did I feel like running away from that place? The problem was that I was dirty inside. My heart was full of unforgiven sin. When they hugged me it "creeped" me out because I was rotten. I was not worthy of such love, God's love! I did not know those people. Why would they want anything to do with me? In my mind, I planned to never go back there again.

The meeting started and there was praise,

worship, and testimonies of what God was doing in the lives of those in attendance. Next came a Bible study and then personal prayer. People stood in a circle holding hands together in a spirit of unity. One by one they prayed as each person talked to God in their own words. They spoke to Jesus just as though he was standing in the center of the circle. The last person in the group gave a final prayer and ended it with Jesus' name.

The meeting ended. I left the same way that I arrived, lost with no purpose to my life. I was a druggy, thief, and a smokin', drinkin', partyin' fool. No job, no money, no goal in life, and I swore that I wasn't going to any more of those prayer meetings. God however still had a plan for my life. He loved me. Out of His love he kept his Holy Spirit chasing after me.

That night we rode home in silence until Dad finally spoke. He asked me if I would go with him to some body's house on the next Wednesday evening for supper. I really didn't want to visit any of Dad's friends, much less have supper with them, but I went to make Dad happy. Little did I know that I was going to be set up. There was going to be a prayer meeting at Betty Amundsen's house on that night and I was going to be the guest of honor.

I will never forget the evening of Wednesday March 4, 1979. There was a supper for five of us. Afterwards, the doorbell rang as others arrived and soon the living room was full of people. The guitars came out and songs of praise filled the air. Next, a fellow by the name of Lloyd Detteine introduced himself as the former police chief of Marshfield, Wisconsin. Lloyd was the featured speaker and I nervously wondered what he was going to talk about. With a Bible in his hand, he testified about the power of a living God. He shared how "All have sinned and fallen short of the glory of God" (Romans 3:23) and he shared how "The wages of sin is death, but the gift of God is eternal life in Christ Jesus" (Romans 6:23). Lloyd then read "God so loved the world that he gave His one and only begotten Son, that whoever believes in him shall not perish but have eternal life" (John 3:16). Going on, he shared how Jesus said, "I am the way and the truth and the life. No one comes to the father except through me" (John 14:6). I perked up at the words "through me." Finally Lloyd shared how God makes it possible for a person to be born again by the power of the Holy Spirit (John 3:5-7).

God's word that night told me that I was a sinner, that the wages for my sin was eternal death and eternal punishment. But I also heard that I could have the gift of eternal life through Jesus Christ. I heard that God the Father was willing that I should not perish and that I could go to heaven through Jesus. I was listening and thinking hard as I heard those Bible passages, and in my heart, I knew they were true. I turned my mind back to what the speaker was saying and heard him recite Revelation 3:20, "Here I am! I stand at the door and knock. If anyone hears my voice and opens the door, I will come in and eat with him, and he with me." The door that was referred to is the door of one's heart.

Lloyd asked me if I would admit to God that I am a sinner and I said yes. He asked me if I understood that I would go to hell if my sins were not forgiven; again I said yes. He asked me if I would be willing to invite Jesus into my life (heart) and be forgiven of my sins. Again I said yes. Lloyd then asked me if I would be willing to repent of (turn from) my wrongful way of living and allow Jesus to guide my life. Again, I said yes.

I had heard about Jesus all of my life in church through the mass but no one ever told me that I could know God personally through Jesus. I jumped at the offer when Lloyd asked me if I wanted a relationship with Jesus. I prayed a sinner's prayer with him. I sat, head bowed, hands together, God's words cut through the apathy of my life, I felt remorse for the first time, for all the wrongful things, the stolen money, the drugs, the lies.This was no repetitious prayer out of a book, it was a prayer of sincerity from the heart.

I invited Jesus to come into my heart, to forgive me and to change me. Now there was no audible voice from Heaven declaring what was happening in me at that moment but I know Jesus entered in and took residence as I offered my heart to him. Immediately my desire to smoke and do drugs was gone.

Instead of being hyper and fidgety I felt peace and warmth. I experienced what Dad had been trying to explain to me about his new life in Jesus. The question I had asked my mother as a twelve year old at bedtime about death was finally answered.

1979

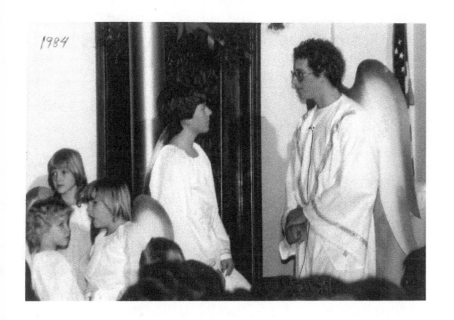

When I received the Lord Jesus into my heart I was giving him permission to help me live my life in a way that is pleasing to Him. From that very night God began a new work in me. I experienced a new birth which the Apostle Paul describes in a letter he wrote to the Corinthians, "Therefore, if anyone is in Christ, he is a new creation; the old has gone, the new has come! All this is from God, who reconciled us to Himself through Christ..." (II Cor. 5:17, 18). I was a new creation! There were still consequences to be paid in my life because of the laws of sowing and reaping. It would be work living a life pleasing to God but with God all things are possible.

The next day the phone rang and when I picked it up I heard the person on the other end of the line say, "Hello, this is Detective Jerry Bartkowiak from the Portage County Sheriff's Department, is this Steven Bornbach? We would like to ask you a few questions." I should have been scared, but I wasn't. I wanted to live a good life and put the past mistakes behind me. Mom had begged me months earlier to "turn myself in and to make restitution for my wrongs," but I ignored her. Now I wanted with all of my heart to let God straighten out all mistakes of my past, all of the wrong choices and all of the wrong attitudes. Within an hour, I was at the Portage County Courthouse.

I knew I might have to pay a price for my past mistakes, but that price was worth being free from all the alcohol, drugs, and meaningless existence.

Detectives Jerry Bartkowiak and Peter Thrun questioned me extensively, and I honestly answered every one of their questions. Questions about the past came up dealing with the stolen car from Carthage, the many burglaries in the area by people, I knew and the perjuring of myself on the witness stand for Don. The confession of my wrongdoing was taped and sent to the D.A. and on July 6, 1979 I went back to court. In the courtroom I once again gave testimony to all questions that were directed to me, however, this time I answered each question honestly.

Since that day in Betty Amundsens house when I opened my heart to God's love, I have walked with Jesus. Many times I have stumbled and fallen, but God continually helps me to get right back up again as he continues his marvelous work in my life. It has been said that Christians are not perfect, just forgiven. I have found that to be true. It is wonderful to know each day that I am forgiven and that my name is written in God's book of life.

Steven Bornbach

14

Chapter Fourteen

For the Skeptics

Remembering back over my own life, I realize there were times of divine intervention before I even knew God. One incident happened while I was working on a dairy farm when I was just sixteen years old. A 700 pound hay wagon platform without wheels was leaning up against the wall of the steel machine shed. My great uncle was nearby shifting equipment around the building and somehow caused the hay wagon's wooden oak platform to begin falling away from the wall. I knew if it tipped just right, it could fall on my great uncle possibly crushing him. Instinctively, I sprang forward from where I was standing and somehow managed to push the massive wooden bed back up against the wall. I realize now that feat should not have been possible for a slender, sixteen year old boy weighing 155 pounds.

Another time of divine intervention took place while I was working in Schaumburg, Illinois in 1977. I was a seventeen year old laborer working on a condominium building project for Lexington Green Corporation. The buildings being constructed were roughed in and roofed but the drywall had not yet been hung. It was customary for us workers to lock up buildings at the end of each day to keep out vandals. This particular evening, I was on one side of the project locking up and Mel Fazio was on the other side of the grounds. As I walked outside from one of the buildings, I heard a loud thud coming from across the courtyard. I looked over from where the sound came from and saw a set of patio doors shaking as from a concussion and heard a scream of pain.

I sprinted to those patio doors as fast as I possibly could. Looking through the open patio door, I could see Mel lying on the concrete floor. Someone in all of their wisdom had piled twenty-seven twelve foot long sheets of drywall against the patio door handles. When Mel went to close the patio doors, the sheet rock fell on him, pinning him to the ground from the knees on down. Without thinking, I charged through the open door and ran over the pile of material to get to Mel. As I did so, he howled in pain and yelled at me for running across the drywall. I responded by asking him what difference a little more weight would make as the pile of sheet rock must have weighed twenty seven hundred pounds. Besides, it was the quickest route to reach him.

I reached down and tried lifting up the pile of sheet rock with my bare hands. Nothing happened when I lifted upward. As hard as I tried, nothing budged. Obviously I was not going to move that pile with my own weak, finite power. In desperation, I asked God to help me and immediately I noticed a small piece of two by four lumber off to my right. The piece of wood was too short to get any real leverage, but I tried it anyway. I jammed one end of the board between the sheet rock and the floor and lifted. The pile raised ever so slightly, just enough for Mel to be able to pull his legs out. That pile of sheetrock weighed nearly 1.5 tons. I do not believe it is possible for a 165 Pound boy to lift that amount of dead weight without the help of God.

I realize the skeptics of this world will say that my stories of the hay wagon bed and the sheet rock are just coincidences. Some folks might say that I had a flow of adrenaline that gave me extra strength. I say it was supernatural strength from a supernatural God.

God continues to be with me. After I became born again, I had an experience that cannot be explained in any way except that God was with me, guiding me and protecting me. This story involves a car, a bus, and fire.

God is Real. He was there. Standing in fire & not burned.

C.L.f. Youth Choir Tour Burnsville, Mn. 1983

It was a hot summer day in 1983. I was with a youth choir group, and we had just finished up a youth choir tour in Farmington, Minnesota. Everyone on the bus was excited to be on their way to Valley Fair near Shakopee, just a short distance away. Our whole group was together except for two girls who were riding with the other youth from the church that hosted us overnight. Those kids were all traveling ahead of our bus in a four door sedan.

Twenty minutes or so into our trip, the bus began going down a large hill. At the bottom of the hill was an intersection with traffic lights. The kids in the sedan in front of us had stopped for a red light. The bus, however, kept barreling forward. The bus driver tried desperately to stop, but the brakes weren't working. The distance between the bus and the car rapidly closed and within seconds, the 38 foot orange bus slammed into the sedan. The car's gas tank ruptured upon impact and burst into fire. The car's steering wheel had been turned all the way to the left in order to make a left turn, so when it was hit, the flaming car thrust forward, spun around, and came back towards the bus, eventually resting alongside the rear wheels on the bus driver's side. The entire car was engulfed in fire and soon the bus began to burn where the car had stopped.

I had been sitting on the passenger side of the bus over the rear wheel when the accident happened. The flaming car caused the kids around me to panic because they wanted out of the bus, but the rear exit was inaccessible due to luggage piled against the door. Some of the kids found a way to crawl out through the windows. For the rest of us, it seemed like an eternity waiting inside the bus as the line of kids exited down the aisle and out through the door. I kept hoping that the bus fuel tank would not catch fire while I was still in the bus. Eventually my turn came. I followed the line from the back of the bus and out through the front door.

Before I left the bus, I turned around to make sure no one else was left inside. It was empty. Outside, everyone grouped together by the curb on the northwest corner of the intersection. Some of the kids seemed to be in shock, eyes wide, speechless. Others were using the local pay phone to call home to their parents. I looked around scanning the huddled group and those by the pay phones and realized that Penelope, my sister, was missing. I shouted her name, as I raced to the other side of the intersection and back around the burning vehicles. No one answered.

That's when I saw her, the form of Penelope through the car door window. She was slumped over, unconscious. The others who had been in the car had run away to safety. No one had stopped to see if anyone else was left inside. Now there was no time to go get help. I raced over to the car. The yellow flames were burning bright and as I got closer, the intense heat forced me to stop when I was about fifteen feet. The force from the impact of the bus had shoved the car's gas tank forward pushing the back right quarter panel into a part of the door that was supposed to open. For a split second I wondered if I was willing to pay the price, to risk burns and injury in an attempt to make the rescue. The second passed. I raced forward determinedly toward the fire. Dressed only in Levi cutoffs and a white tee shirt, I struggled to get the jammed door open but it would not budge. Witnesses said that on my second effort I jerked the door open.

I somehow reached in through the flames and pulled Penelope from the car and carried her to the curb. Minutes later, the ambulance came and took her to Hennepin County Medical Center in Minneapolis where she was treated for a broken jaw and other medical trauma. Looking back on this incident, I can say with certainty that God was with me in the fire. Some people might want to argue that fact. People might say that ripping the door open was merely a flow of adrenaline. I know differently. God was with me and Penelope that day, saving both of us from the fire.

I know this because there was another unexplainable incident which also occurred that day as the fire totally consumed the car. Inside the car was a plastic key tag with the word Jesus written on it. This plastic key tag survived the flames, survived the heat. It never melted. There was also a Bible in the car where the plastic key tag was found. The pages of the Bible were not burned even though everything else in the car was consumed by fire. Those events cannot be explained! Yes, God was definitely there! And yes, God still works miracles for those willing to have faith that doesn't burn!

There are three other times that I can share of when God had proven his great power in my life. A few years after I was born again in Christ, one of my sons was born. It was common for my young family to come and visit me while I worked as a custodian at Bethlehem Lutheran Church. One day I was cleaning the preschool area in the basement when my one year old son fell and hit his head on the thinly carpeted cement floor. A patch of blood appeared and began growing just under the skin of his fine blond hair. I immediately prayed for him to be healed in the name of Jesus. The blotch under the skin disappeared while I prayed. What appeared to be pooling blood beneath the scalp disappeared. I am not anyone special, but I am a son of God through Christ Jesus. God helps his sons and daughters when they cry out to him. I believe he helped my son that day.

Another time, I had left the house to go to work at 4:30 A.M to perform snow removal at the church. I made sure the house door was locked behind me as I left my sleeping wife down stairs in our bedroom and our two sleeping boys upstairs. Soon thereafter, my wife was awakened from her deep sleep by a loud male voice in the house. The voice told her to go upstairs and check on our new born son. Thinking the voice was mine, Jean hollered for me to go upstairs and check on the boys myself. She then started falling back asleep but was awakened by the voice once again. Jean thinking I was being lazy was fuming. She got out of bed and marched her way up the stairs. As she entered the baby's room, she found the baby with his face buried in the bumper of the crib, struggling to breath. Was the male voice or the timing of the event a coincidence? I don't think so. God called out to Jean and because she listened, our son was saved.

I believe this, God not only watches over all of us, but he gives us authority through him. Evidence of this occurred years back when my new family had just moved into an old two story house on the highway. Strange sounds periodically emanated from upstairs on the second floor when no one was up there. The sounds were unnerving seemingly occurring from nothing. We spoke with the land lord about our concerns. She told us that a woman once lived in our house who people thought was a witch and the alleged witch once had a baby that mysteriously died in our home. One night we were in our house watching television when we heard activity beginning upstairs. Once again we could hear sounds, but this time the sounds were much louder than before. We heard what sounded like a large bowling ball rolling over a hard tile or wooden floor, yet the floors upstairs were all covered with carpet.

Obviously the activity was a paranormal phenomenon in our house and I suspected that it was the
result of demonic activity. The only available course
of action to combat such forces was to go throughout
all of the house rebuking the spirits in the name of
Jesus and to plead the blood of Jesus in and over our
home and property to drive the demons out.

So I did. I went upstairs and walked from room
to room rebuking the spirits in the name of Jesus
and commanded them to leave. Then I pleaded the
blood of Jesus over our entire house and property.
The sounds ceased. From that day on our house was
quiet, safe and secure; the noises never came back.

I believe there are supernatural influences on
mankind. Too often the unexplainable occurs. Just
as there are forces of good, the forces of darkness
are out to deceive, disrupt, and confuse anyone who
is gullible to go along with their antics. God's power
however, is greater than evil. In the name of Jesus
today's believers have authority to rebuke and overcome the forces of evil.

Many misguided people today are skeptical
when hearing about miracles. It does not matter
whether they are "religious" or not. Even people in
mainline denominations believe miracles died out
two thousand years ago with the twelve disciples of
Jesus. God says differently in the book of Hebrews
13:8 which says, "Jesus is the same yesterday, today
and forever." The same Jesus of yesteryear is still

working in the affairs of mankind today. Anyone who tries to limit God's ability to help and to heal is only cheating themselves out of God's many blessings.

15

Chapter Fifteen

Would You like to know Jesus?

The first fourteen chapters of this book were about life experiences leading up to my salvation experience. This chapter is an opportunity for you the reader to decide whether you will receive Jesus into your own life; the choice is yours.

Either you know God or you do not. Is it presumptuous to say that you can know whether you are going to heaven? No, it is not presumptuous. The Bible gives assurances to anyone willing to read them. Romans 10: 9, 10, "If you confess with your mouth, Jesus is Lord, and believe in your heart that God raised Him from the dead, you will be saved. For it is with your heart that you believe and are justified, and it is with your mouth that you confess and are saved." Note that you must believe with your heart and confess with your mouth.

The bible says that we can know Christ that we can be found in him when he becomes our righteousness:

> But whatever was to my profit I now
> consider loss for the sake of Christ. What
> is more, I consider everything a loss
> compared to the surpassing greatness of
> knowing Christ Jesus my Lord, for whose
> sake I have lost all things. I consider
> them rubbish, that I may gain Christ and
> be found in him, not having a righteous-
> ness of my own that comes from the law,
> but that which is through faith in Christ –
> the righteousness that comes from God
> and is by faith - Phil. 3:7 – 9.

God's word says that we can receive eternal life but that life comes only through his son, "This is the testimony: God has given us eternal life, and this life is in his son. He who has the son has life; he who does not have the Son of God does not have life "– 1 John 5:11 – 12.

He who has the son has life. How much plainer can God say that we definitely have eternal life if we receive it through Jesus?

It is important to be aware that God keeps books and those books will one day be opened in God's presence. One of those books is the book of life, and your name is written in that book the moment you receive Jesus into your heart. The book of Revelation in the Bible describes the following:

Then I saw a great white throne and him
who was seated on it. Earth and sky fled
from his presence, and there was no
place for them. And I saw the dead, great
and small, standing before the throne,
and the books were opened. Another
book was opened, which is the book of
life. The dead were judged according to
what they had done as recorded in the
books. The sea gave up the dead that
were in it, and death and Hades gave up
the dead that were in them. And each
person was judged according to what he
had done. Then death and Hades were
thrown into the lake of fire. The lake
of fire is the second death. If anyone's
name was not found written in the book
of life, he was thrown into the lake of fire
- Revelation 20: 11 – 15.

Note that if anyone's name is not found written
in the book of life, they will be thrown into the lake of
fire.

There are many "religious" people today who
do not know God. They believe that going to church
makes them a Christian. Going to church will not
make you any more of a Christian than going to Mc-
Donalds would cause you to become a hamburger.
There are undoubtedly some poor souls determined
to get to heaven their own way. Are they ever going

to be shocked when they pound on the door of heaven and are not allowed in because their life was not found in Jesus.

There are examples in the Bible of very good religious people who realized their need of a savior and who turned their lives over to Jesus:

> Philip met an Ethiopian eunuch, an important official in charge of all the treasury of Candace, queen of the Ethiopians. This man had gone to Jerusalem to worship, and on his way home was sitting in his chariot reading the book of Isaiah the prophet. Philip ran up to the chariot and heard the man reading Isaiah the prophet. Do you understand what you are reading?" Philip asked. "How can I," he said, "unless someone explains it to me? The eunuch asked Philip," Tell me please, who is the prophet talking about, himself or someone else?" Then Philip began with that very verse of scripture and told him the good news about Jesus; after the eunuch believed he was baptized - Acts 8:26 – 40.

The eunuch was so religious that he traveled over 600 miles to worship God in Jerusalem. Yet this man realized that he was lacking the one ingredient needed for salvation: Jesus. It was not merely enough for the eunuch to travel a great distance to worship

God; the man had to receive Jesus!

In Acts chapter nine, we find another very religious man by the name of Saul. Saul obeyed every law of the Torah (Old Testament) and was a very devout Pharisee. He traveled to Damascus one day and encountered Jesus (Acts 9:4-6). Saul turned his life over to Jesus, later received the Holy Spirit, and was healed of temporary blindness. In becoming a new creation through Jesus, Saul's name was changed to Paul; who went on to become the apostle Paul.

Both the eunuch and Saul were devoutly religious and yet they realized that they must place their faith, hope, and trust in Jesus to be saved. Have you ever surrendered your life to Jesus or do you need to re - dedicate your life to him? Is something holding you back? You have nothing to lose and everything to gain by asking Jesus into your heart. Are you willing to let Jesus forgive you of all your sins? Are you willing to trust him with your life from this day forward? No one has a guarantee of tomorrow. Please do not let this moment of opportunity pass you by. Hebrews 3:15 says "If today you hear his voice, harden not your heart."

Why not take a moment right now to ask Jesus into your life? You can use your own words to pray or use the following example: "Dear Heavenly Father, You have called me to yourself in the name of your dear Son Jesus. I realize that Jesus is the only way, the truth, and the life, and is the only mediator between you and man. I acknowledge to you that I am a sinner. I believe that your only begotten Son Jesus Christ shed his precious blood on the cross, died for my sins, and rose again on the third day. I am truly sorry for the deeds which I have committed against you; therefore, I am willing to turn away from my sins. Have mercy on me, a sinner. Cleanse me and forgive me of my sins as I forgive anyone who has ever sinned against me. I truly desire to serve you, Lord Jesus. Starting from now, I pray that you would help me to hear your still small voice. Lord, I desire to be led by your Holy Spirit so I can faithfully follow you and obey all of your commandments. I ask you for the strength to love you more than anything else so I will not fall back into my old ways. I also ask you to bring genuine believers into my life who will encourage me to live for you and help me to stay accountable. Lord Jesus please transform my life so that I may bring glory and honor to you alone and not to myself. Right now I confess Jesus as Lord of my life. With my heart I believe that God the Father raised his Son Jesus from the dead. This very moment I acknowledge that Jesus Christ is my Savior and according to his word, right now, I am born again. Thank you, Jesus, for coming into my life and hearing my prayer. I ask all of this in the name of my Lord and Savior, Jesus Christ. Amen.

I congratulate anyone who took the time to sincerely offer their life to Jesus. All of heaven rejoices with you, "In the same way, I tell you, there is rejoicing in the presence of the angels of God over one sinner who repents" - Luke 15:10. God loves you so much and wants to help you live for him.

Right now I must first prepare you to stand firm in Christ Jesus because there are three obstacles standing in the way of victory in your daily living. There is the way of the world with its ungodliness; there is our very own humanity, or flesh, that does not always want to do God's will; there is a rotten devil who wants to trip us up in hopes that we will give up on God. The devil is not happy that you became a son or daughter of God. You are a threat to him when you walk with God, read God's word, and pray. You must develop a faith that does not burn up and become a lifeless pile of ash. You need a faith that overcomes and perseveres through the storms of this life.

The devil will try deceive you into thinking your experience with Jesus is not real. Rebuke those thoughts and pray to Jesus as you seek his word daily for strength. God's word, the Bible, is our most potent weapon in overcoming the Wiley schemes of the devil. God's prescription for us to overcome the devil is found in the book of Ephesians:

> Finally, be strong in the Lord and in his mighty power. Put on the full armor of God, so that you can take your stand against the devil's schemes. For our struggle is not against flesh and blood, but against the rulers, against the au-

thorities, against the powers of this dark world and against the spiritual forces of evil in the heavenly realms. Therefore put on the full armor of God, so that when the day of evil comes, you may be able to stand your ground, and after you have done everything, to stand. Stand firm then, with the belt of truth buckled around your waist, with the breastplate of righteousness in place, and with your feet fitted with the readiness that comes from the gospel of peace. In addition to all this, take up the shield of faith, with which you can extinguish all the flaming arrows of the evil one. Take the helmet of salvation and the sword of the Spirit, which is the word of God. And pray in the Spirit on all occasions with all kinds of prayers and requests – Ephesians 6: 10 – 18.

You have to keep on guard against the devil and his schemes, but you also must not let the cares of this world consume you. The cares and troubles of this world will try and choke you off, like weeds in a garden trying to overtake the vegetables. You can overcome these trials by finding a church that preaches the whole gospel. Remember, people are not perfect and neither are churches. Find dependable, trustworthy Christians to fellowship with, to become grounded in God's word and to become strong in your faith.

I have found the biggest enemy to accomplishing what God wants for my life is myself, my selfishness, and doing what I want. Jesus willingly gave himself up to do his father's will and we must be willing to do the same. One of the greatest examples of faith that could not be destroyed, or "burned up" so to speak, was the apostle Paul. He struggled with subjecting his body to the will of the Holy Spirit when he first became born again. Eventually, Paul was able to overcome adversity through submission to the Holy Spirit. This takes a lot of time and patience. It is a process that we must work out all the days of our life. Paul describes his initial frustrations with his inadequacies before learning to depend on the Holy Spirit:

> I know that nothing good lives in me,
> that is, in my sinful nature. For I have the
> desire to do what is good, but I cannot
> carry it out. For what I do is not the good
> I want to do; no, the evil I do not want
> to do – this I keep on doing. Now if I do
> what I do not want to do, it is no longer
> I who do it, but it is sin living in me that
> does it. So I find this law at work: when I
> want to do good, evil is right there with
> me. For in my inner being I delight in
> God's law; but I see another law at work
> in the members of my body, waging war

> against the law of my mind and making
> me a prisoner of the law of sin at work
> within my members. What a wretched
> man I am! Who will rescue me from
> this body of death? Thanks be to God –
> through Jesus Christ our Lord! – Romans
> 7: 18 – 25.

I realize that the scripture you just read sounds complicated, so let me simplify it this way. Paul did not feel like doing what was right every day. However, God's spirit dwelt within him to help Paul do what was right. Through daily prayer, Paul was able to overcome his shortcomings. The book of Romans has more good news. We do not have to beat ourselves up or condemn ourselves each time that we make a mistake:

> Therefore, there is now no longer con-
> demnation for those who are in Christ
> Jesus, because through Christ Jesus the
> law of the Spirit of life set me free from
> the law of sin and death. For what the
> law was powerless to do in that it was
> weakened by the sinful nature, God did
> by sending his own Son in the likeness
> of sinful man to be a sin offering. And so
> he condemned sin in sinful man, in order
> that the righteous requirements of the
> law might be fully met in us, who do not
> live according to the sinful nature but

according to the Spirit – Romans 8:1-4.

A summary of that scripture is that God's law in the Old Testament showed us all of his requirements that were impossible to completely obey. However, through the perfect sacrifice of Jesus death and resurrection from the cross, all requirements were met for us when we invited Jesus into our lives to take away our sin. Simply put, Jesus' blood washes away all of our imperfections each time we fail or make mistakes. There will be some failures on our part in this life but the important thing is to ask God's forgiveness each time we fail and get right back up to live lives that are pleasing to him. God's comforter, the Holy Spirit, is able to help us do what we otherwise could not do in our own power.

Steven Bornbach

16

Chapter Sixteen

Faith that doesn't burn

We must never give up on our faith in God. We must not allow discouragement to overcome us. We must be committed to prayer at all times. There are going to be times when you feel like your prayers are not being answered, but rest assured, God hears your pleas. God is moving even when it seems like you think he isn't.

Many times over the years I have heard people ask why it seems to take so long for God to answer their prayers. The answer is God is never early, he is never late, and God is always right on time. There is another factor why our prayers appear to be lacking speedy results and that is our lack of prayer. It has been said that prayer moves the hands of God so how can we expect results if we do not pray?

Prayer is critical to winning wars in the heavenlies which affect the outcome of our spiritual battles here on earth. The battles can be likened to a game of chess with the king, queen, bishop, knight, rook and pawns. The dark side has Satan, one third of the fallen angels or demons, and their horde of principalities and powers led by a demonic government of hierarchy. This is explained in Ephesians 6:12.

The good guys in the battle are God Almighty who is infallible and cannot fail in any of his plans. He is all knowing, all powerful, and everywhere. God the Son and God the Holy Spirit have their roles to play. Together they all make the Holy Trinity, the three in one. Joining their team are two thirds of the angels who remained faithful to God when Satan tried to overthrow him. This account of mutiny can be found in Ezekiel 28.

Each of the spiritual forces on both sides of this invisible war have their own strategies being worked out through people and circumstances here on earth. Unseen forces are trying to fight and to block one another to keep their opponents from winning the war for the souls of mankind. Many verses in the Bible attest to this great struggle but one passage in the book of Daniel makes this concept easy to understand:

> A hand touched me and set me trembling on my hands and knees. He said, "Daniel, you who are highly esteemed, consider carefully the words I am about to speak to you, and stand up, for I have been sent to you." And when he said this to me I stood up trembling. Then he continued, "Do not be afraid, Daniel. Since the first day that you set your mind to gain understanding and to

humble yourself before your God, your words were heard, and I have come in response to them. But the prince of the Persian Kingdom resisted me twenty – one days. Then Michael one of the chief princes, came to help me, because I was detained there with the kind of Persia – Dan. 10:10 – 13.

What we learn from these verses is that as soon as Daniel prayed God heard him. Immediately God sent an angelic messenger to answer Daniel's prayer. However, the princes of evil tried to keep the answer to prayer from reaching Daniel. Do not lose heart if your prayers do not seem to get answered quickly. God will answer your prayers and your need will be met in God's perfect time.

In this life we may be asked by people in this world to do things that blatantly disobey God's directives. We may have to pay a price for our faith when we choose to obey God rather that the commands of men. God will be with us through those fiery trials of testing as our obedience to him is tested.

As believers, we can learn from the example of three young men who were ordered to worship a golden statue rather than worship the God of Heaven. The men chose to obey the God of Heaven rather than the orders of men. As a penalty for disobedience, the men were sent to die in a fiery furnace. Not only did God protect the men who were thrown into that blazing furnace but Daniel says God stood with them in the fire:

> He said, "Look! I see four men walk-
> ing around in the fire, unbound and
> unharmed, and the fourth looks like a
> son of the gods." Nebuchadnezzar then
> approached the opening of the blazing
> furnace and shouted, "Shadrach, Me-
> shach and Abednego, servants of the
> Most High God, come out! Come here."

> So Shadrach, Meshach and Abednego
> came out of the fire, and the satraps,
> prefects, governors and royal advisors
> crowded around them. They saw that
> the fire had not harmed their bodies, nor
> was a hair of their heads singed; their
> robes were not scorched and there was
> no smell of fire on them – Dan. 3:25-27.

We are not always delivered from trials or hardship. Sometimes we must go through them. Jesus himself did not turn from his mission of being beaten and crucified on a cross. He endured pain and suffering to make salvation available to all mankind. Jesus never wanted to suffer yet he obeyed the will of his father even though it meant death. The book of 1 Peter reveals how suffering, grief, and trials, are used by God to perfect our faith in him:

> In this you greatly rejoice, though now

for a little while you may have had to suffer grief in all kinds of trials. These have come so that your faith – of greater worth than gold, which perishes even though refined by fire – may be proved genuine and may result in praise, glory and honor when Jesus Christ is revealed.

Humble yourselves, under God's mighty hand, that he may lift you up in due time. Cast all your anxiety on him because he cares for you. Be self-controlled and alert. Your enemy the devil prowls around like a roaring lion looking for someone to devour. Resist him standing firm in the faith, because you know that your brothers throughout the world are undergoing the same kind of sufferings – 1 Pet. 1:6, 7, 5:6 -9.

Even the apostle Peter went through adversity, "Jesus said Simon, Simon, Satan has asked to sift you as wheat" – Luke 22:31. Satan tried to sift or trip up Peter the night Jesus was arrested in the garden of Gethsemane. That same night Peter denied Jesus three times before the cock crowed. Do not be surprised when the devil tries to shake your faith. Always be on your guard against the wiles of the Devil as there will be testing in the life of every believer, "Everyone will be salted with fire" – Mark 9:49.

Steven Bornbach

Loosely interpreted, every Christian in this life can expect to undergo the fire of suffering and persecution as we see in the book of 1 Peter:

> "Dear friends, do not be surprised at the painful trial you are suffering, as though something strange were happening to you. But rejoice that you participate in the sufferings of Christ, so that you may be overjoyed when his glory is revealed. If you are insulted because of the name of Christ, you are blessed, for the Spirit of glory and of God rests on you... If you suffer as a Christian, do not be ashamed, but praise God that you bear that name – 1 Pet. 4:12 -14, 16.

Now, I cannot say that I have faith that doesn't burn. I am not there yet, but I pray for the Holy Spirit to help me should that time come. The apostle Paul suffered tremendously and yet he was able to pen the following words as an encouragement for us. Paul states in Romans that Jesus himself is interceding for us that our faith will stand firm:

> Christ Jesus who died – more than that, who was raised to life – is at the right hand of God and is also interceding for us. Who shall separate us from the love of Christ? Shall trouble or hardship or persecution or famine or nakedness or danger or sword? No, in all things we

216

are more than conquerors through him who loved us. For I am convinced that neither death nor life, neither angels nor demons, neither the present nor the future, nor any powers, neither heights nor depth, nor anything else in all creation, will be able to separate us from the love of God that is in Christ Jesus our Lord – Rom. 8:34, 35, 37 – 39.

You may be asking yourself if being faithful to Jesus is worth the cost; it is. Remember, Jesus left his throne of glory to take your place on a cross that was meant for you. In exchange, he offers to you eternal life forever in paradise.

The following scriptures show great rewards for those who persevere, endure and overcome the difficulties of this life for Jesus' sake:

For everyone born of God overcomes the world. This is the victory that has overcome the world, even our faith. Who is it that overcomes the world? Only he who believes that Jesus is the Son of God – 1 John 5:4, 5.

He who has an ear, let him hear what the Spirit says to the churches. To him who overcomes, I will give the right to eat from the tree of life, which is in the paradise of God... He who has an ear, let him hear what the Spirit says to the churches. He who overcomes will not be hurt at all by the second death – Rev. 2:7, 11.

He who overcomes will, like them, be dressed in white. I will never blot out his name from the book of life, but will acknowledge his name before my Father and his angels... To him who overcomes I will make a pillar in the temple of my God. Never again will he leave it. I will write on him the name of my God and the name of the city of my God, the new Jerusalem, which is coming down out of heaven from my God; and I will also write on him my new name... To him who overcomes, I will give the right to sit with me on my throne, just as I overcame and sat down with my Father on his throne – Rev. 3:5, 12, 21.

He said to me: It is done. I am the alpha and the Omega, the Beginning and the End. To him who is thirsty I will give to drink without cost from the spring of the water of life. He who overcomes will inherit all of this, and I will be his God and he will be my son – Rev. 21: 6, 7.

In closing, may our words someday be the same as the Apostle Paul's in the book of Timothy, "Now I have fought the good fight, I have finished the race, I have kept the faith. Now there is in store for me the crown of righteousness, which the Lord, the righteous Judge, will award to me, but also to all who have longed for his appearing – 1 Tim. 4:7.

Steven Bornbach

Acknowledgements

I am deeply indebted to the many people who encouraged me in the writing of this book as it progressed. Perhaps it would not be written today if it were not for Kathleen Esser, Bonita Folz, Bev Steinke, Sandy Kautzer, Mark Frisch, Teresa Bornbach, Caleb Bornbach, David Bornbach, Lea Ann Turner, Jason Planer, Robert O'Connor, Matthew Schneider, Richelle Hoekstra Anderson, Sandra Nichols and others.

Special thanks to Jason Planer and Lea Ann Turner for their expertise and technical advice on how to put this book together and to Sandra Nichols for her awesome skills in editing.

They say that our life is God's gift to us and what we do with our life is our gift back to God. Thank you Jesus for giving me your life, please use this book to your glory. Amen

Steven Bornbach

About the Author

Steve Bornbach currently lives in the central Wisconsin township of Grand Rapids with his faithful companion Max, an eight year old black Lab. Having been a custodian for thirty two years, Steve is currently setting his sights on retirement in the not too distant future. His dream is to one day purchase property on the beloved 'Seven Mile Creek' in which to live out the 'golden years.' In the meantime, there are children and grandchildren to visit. His long range plans are to take even more trips around the country with his dad and Uncle Alvin.

There are many more projects listed on Steve's bucket list that he would like to accomplish. One project is to write a book titled, "Looking at Saratoga." Another is to organize hundreds of pages of European church records from the 1800's that are located in his museum and use them to show how people in central Wisconsin are related. At any rate, Steve will not be idle. This book was a great 'ride' and Steve feels most fortunate to have written it.

CPSIA information can be obtained
at www.ICGtesting.com
Printed in the USA
FSHW010222230621
82608FS